****

ENGLISH PRONUNCIATION FOR SPANISH SPEAKERS: Consonants

****

PAULETTE DALE, Ph.D.

Miami-Dade Community College

LILLIAN POMS, M.Ed.

Hearing and Speech Center of Florida, Inc.

PRENTICE HALL REGENTS
Englewood Cliffs, New Jersey 07632

Library of Congress Cataloging-in-Publication Data

Dale, Paulette.
    English pronunciation for Spanish speakers—
consonants.

    1. English language—Text-books for foreign
speakers—Spanish.   2. English language—United
States—Pronunciation.   3. English language—
Consonants.   I. Poms, Lillian.   II. Title.
PE1129.S8D15 1986   428.3'461   86-81
ISBN 0-13-281304-1 (pbk.)

Cover design: Ben Santora
Manufacturing buyer: Harry P. Baisley

 © 1986 by Prentice Hall Regents
Prentice-Hall, Inc.
A Paramount Communications Company
Englewood Cliffs, New Jersey 07632

Printed in the United States of America

20   19   18   17   16   15   14

ISBN 0-13-281304-1   01

PRENTICE-HALL INTERNATIONAL (UK) LIMITED, *London*
PRENTICE-HALL OF AUSTRALIA PTY. LIMITED, *Sydney*
PRENTICE-HALL CANADA INC., *Toronto*
PRENTICE-HALL HISPANOAMERICANA, S.A., *Mexico*
PRENTICE-HALL OF INDIA PRIVATE LIMITED, *New Delhi*
PRENTICE-HALL OF JAPAN, INC., *Tokyo*
PRENTICE-HALL OF SOUTHEAST ASIA PTE. LTD., *Singapore*
EDITORA PRENTICE-HALL DO BRASIL, LTDA., *Rio de Janeiro*

CONTENTS

iii

TO THE TEACHER   *175*

APPENDIX   *190*
SPANISH STUDY GUIDE   *225*

```
***************************************
```

PREFACE

```
***************************************
```

For many years the authors have been teaching accent reduction classes composed largely of native Spanish speakers. We find that most of the available American English pronunciation texts are not directed to the particular problems of Spanish speakers and are too technical and confusing for self-teaching.

Our students always request material and tapes for home use. For this reason, we have developed a program for self-study composed of two manuals and cassette tapes. The program is specifically directed to the Spanish speaker (although it can be effectively used by <u>any</u> nonnative speaker of English) who wants to reduce his or her accent when speaking English.

This **English Pronunciation for Spanish Speakers** program is a unique method of instruction. It consists of the following two parts, each of which may be purchased independently:

> *English Pronunciation for Spanish Speakers:* ***Consonants***
> *English Pronunciation for Spanish Speakers:* ***Vowels***

```
***************************************
```

ACKNOWLEDGMENTS

```
***************************************
```

The authors wish to express their sincerest gratitude to the many people who have helped develop this program:

Professor Tommie Ems of the College of Lake County, Susan Epstein of the Hearing and Speech Center of Florida, the teachers who helped field test the materials and recommended valuable improvements.

Professor David Gravel, Director of Broadcasting at Miami Dade Community College for producing the audio cassettes and for his great role as "instructor on the tape."

TEACHERS: Please skip ahead to **To the Teacher** on page 175.

Lisette M. Betancourt of the Hearing and Speech Center of Florida for generously offering to translate the Study Guide into Spanish.

Allan Poms, Jerry Dale, and the rest of our families for their support and encouragement throughout.

But most important of all, we are grateful and indebted to our students, past, present, and future, for using this program, for encouraging us, and for giving us many practical suggestions to help better meet their needs.

✳✳✳✳✳✳✳✳✳✳✳✳✳✳✳✳✳✳✳✳✳✳✳✳✳✳✳✳✳✳✳✳✳✳✳✳✳
AUDIO CASSETTE TAPE OUTLINE
✳✳✳✳✳✳✳✳✳✳✳✳✳✳✳✳✳✳✳✳✳✳✳✳✳✳✳✳✳✳✳✳✳✳✳✳✳

TAPE 1

****

AUDIO CASSETTE TAPE OUTLINE *(cont'd.)*

****

TAPE 2

```
*************************************
```
INTRODUCTION
```
*************************************
```

Welcome to *English Pronunciation for Spanish Speakers.* Before we begin, we'd like to discuss "foreign accents" in general. The dictionary defines *accent* as "speech habits typical of the natives of a region." This means that **we all** have accents!

You should be PROUD of having an accent. Yes, we said **proud!** A foreign accent tells listeners that you speak at least **two** languages. That certainly puts you far ahead of a person who can speak only one language. Besides, the world would be very dull if we all sounded the same. After all, *variety is the spice of life!*

Unfortunately, there is a disadvantage to having a foreign accent. It may hinder effective communication in your nonnative language and cause you to be misunderstood. Our main goal is to help you improve your pronunciation of American English. This will enable you to communicate clearly exactly what you want to say. *We will be with you throughout this book to help you along the way!*

Please turn the page and continue reading. The next section is **not** for teachers; it is **especially for you!**

****

TO THE STUDENT

****

You bought **English Pronunciation for Spanish Speakers** because you feel a need to improve your oral ability to speak English as a second language. We know it is frustrating to have someone say, "I can't understand you because of your accent." We also know that you might be afraid to use certain words because you'll mispronounce them. Many of our students avoid words like *sheet* and *beach*. Instead they ask for a *piece* of paper and say they went to the *ocean*. We understand your feelings and want to reassure you. Please don't worry! You don't have to avoid saying certain words and phrases or to be misunderstood by other people.

English Pronunciation for Spanish Speakers: Consonants has been written especially for you. You will soon find that this program has been designed to help you overcome your particular pronunciation problems when speaking English and that it is an independent program you can use on your own. The manual is written in easy-to-understand terms and is accompanied by cassette tapes to help you learn to pronounce the American-English consonants correctly. You don't need a teacher (or speech therapist) to use this program.

English Pronunciation for Spanish Speakers: Consonants covers the various consonant sounds in the English language. Each chapter follows a specific format and contains the following sections:

PRONOUNCING THE SOUND . . .

A simple explanation of how to pronounce the consonant is given. Details for actual placement of the articulators (lips, tongue, etc.) are discussed.

SPANISH KEY WORDS . . .

Spanish key words with the equivalent English consonant are provided. These give you a familiar sound with which to relate.

POSSIBLE PRONUNCIATION PROBLEMS
FOR THE SPANISH SPEAKER . . .

This section explains why the consonant creates problems for you and how your pronunciation difficulties are related to specific differences between Spanish and English.

HINTS . . .

A series of rules to help you remember when to produce the sound are provided. They will help you use English spelling patterns as a guide to pronunciation.

EXERCISES . . .

This section has a variety of exercises designed to give you comprehensive practice with the consonant sound as it occurs in words, common phrases, and sentences.

SELF-TESTS . . .

This section contains mini-tests to help you evaluate your progress. Your ability to recognize and pronounce the sound in words, sentences, and conversational activities will be tested.

FOR AN ENCORE . . .

This section is designed to give you practice in using the target consonant in daily life. A variety of listening, reading, and conversational activities are provided at the end of each chapter.

Additional chapters include explanations and exercises for the correct pronunciation of past tense verbs and plural nouns. Answers to all self-test items are given in the Appendix.

The audio tapes that accompany the manual contain recorded sections of each chapter (these are clearly marked in the manual) and are designed to provide a model of correct pronunciation for each sound covered. Please refer to page vi for a complete outline of the material included on the cassette tapes.

USING THE *ENGLISH PRONUNCIATION FOR SPANISH SPEAKERS PROGRAM*

Now you are ready to begin the program. The only other materials you will need are a cassette recorder to play the tapes and a mirror to help you correctly place your articulators to make the right sound. Find yourself a quiet, comfortable area to practice in; bring along your enthusiasm and determination to improve your speech—*and you're all ready to go!*

Before beginning the program, read Chapter 1 in the manual and play Tape 1 (Side A) completely to become familiar with the format of the lessons. (Be sure you understand the written explanations in the manual before beginning oral practice.)

EXERCISES . . .

Rewind the tape to the beginning and look at Exercise A, Chapter 1 (page vi). Practice the exercise by using the directions provided. Repeat the words after the instructor during the pauses. You can stop the tape whenever you like and repeat a section. If you have difficulty at any time, stop the tape and reread the directions for pronouncing the consonant. Look in the mirror to be sure your articulators are in the correct position. Continue with each exercise until you feel you can say the words and sentences easily. Before starting the next section, you should be able to repeat the material after the instructor on the tape without looking at the book.

SELF-TESTS . . .

After you are satisfied with your ability to do the exercises, begin the self-tests. The instructions for each self-test are different; read all the directions carefully before beginning. When you finish each test, turn off the recorder and check your answers in the Appendix. If you have any difficulty with the tests, return to the beginning of the chapter and repeat the exercises. The dialogues and paragraphs are the most difficult activities in each chapter; review them often as you progress through the manual.

FOR AN ENCORE . . .

When you're content with your pronunciation of the target consonant in the exercises and self-tests, you are ready to progress from the book to "real life" situations. These are only a few suggestions to guide you in making your correct pronunciation of the sound automatic. Try to find other ways to incorporate the sound into your daily routine.

REVIEW CHAPTERS . . .

Review chapters are designed to give additional practice. Complete the self-tests as you did in the previous chapters. If you have difficulty with one of the consonants, return to the appropriate chapter and review.

PRACTICE SESSIONS . . .

It is very important to practice as much as possible. Try to follow a definite time schedule. Daily practice sessions are ideal, but if your time is limited, try to practice at least three or four times a week (even if only for 20 to 30 minutes). *We know that reading the book and listening to the tapes is very hard work.* **TAKE A BREAK WHEN YOU GET TIRED.** Continue your study session when you feel refreshed. DON'T TRY TO DO IT ALL AT ONCE! **Improvement takes time. But little by little you will succeed!**

Keep your tape recorder and cassettes handy to use in the kitchen while you are preparing dinner or in the car while you're driving to work. Practice when you're relaxed, rested, and motivated so you will do your very best. *PRACTICE MAKES PERFECT!*

OTHER WAYS TO IMPROVE YOUR SPEECH

Listening to correct pronunciation patterns is as important as practicing them. Take advantage of as many opportunities as possible to hear English being spoken correctly. You can do this by following these suggestions:

1. Watch the evening news on television. Pay careful attention to the newscaster's pronunciation of words. Repeat some of the words and phrases aloud. (*Your family won't think you are talking to yourself! They'll admire you for trying to improve.*)

2. Listen to radio news stations for five or ten minutes at a time. Repeat common words and phrases after the announcer. *(If anyone gives you a strange look, just tell them you are practicing your speech!)*

3. When one of your favorite television shows is on, try to understand the dialogue without watching, *or* if you must keep your eyes glued to the screen every minute, wait for the commercials to practice your listening skills without watching.

4. Converse frequently with native American-English speakers.

5. Ask your listeners if you are pronouncing a specific word correctly. *They will be glad to help!*

6. **Most important of all—BE BRAVE!** The exercises are full of common expressions. Use some of them in real conversations. For example, *Easy does it* or *It's a pleasure to meet you* are common phrases you can easily practice. No one will realize that you are doing your homework!

Although this program emphasizes pronunciation, the material used in the manual can help you increase your vocabulary. When you don't understand a word or idiom, look it up in the dictionary. Write the definition in your manual so you won't forget it.

You might be wondering how long it will take before you actually see some improvement in your speech. We believe that **English Pronunciation for Spanish Speakers** provides you with everything you need to improve your speech. If you follow the program as it is outlined, you should notice an improvement in just a few weeks. ***Remember—THE MORE YOU PRACTICE, THE FASTER YOU WILL IMPROVE!***

Motivation really can contribute to changes in speech. Many aspiring actors and actresses have lost heavy accents in order to become movie stars. We can't guarantee you a movie contract, but we know that following this program will help you to be better understood and to communicate better in your everyday lives. Good luck!

READ ON AND LET'S GET STARTED!

✳✳✳✳✳✳✳✳✳✳✳✳✳✳✳✳✳✳✳✳✳✳✳✳✳✳✳✳✳✳✳✳✳✳✳
A KEY TO PRONOUNCING
THE CONSONANTS
OF AMERICAN ENGLISH
✳✳✳✳✳✳✳✳✳✳✳✳✳✳✳✳✳✳✳✳✳✳✳✳✳✳✳✳✳✳✳✳✳✳✳

You have probably discovered that there is a big difference between the way words are spelled in English and how they are pronounced. English spelling patterns are inconsistent and are not always a reliable guide to pronunciation. For example, in the following words, the letters ch are used to represent **three** different sounds.

machine   chain   mechanic

Pretty confusing, right? That's why we need a set of symbols in which **each** sound is represented by a **different** symbol. In this program, you will learn the International Phonetic Alphabet (IPA), which is used all over the world. It consists of a set of symbols in which **one symbol** always represents **one sound.**

Many modern dictionaries use the IPA in addition to a system of symbols known as *diacritical marks* to help you pronounce words. Since you frequently refer to a dictionary when reading and speaking English, we have included the most common dictionary equivalents of the IPA symbols.

DON'T WORRY! It won't be necessary to learn all the symbols at once. Each consonant will be introduced and explained **one at a time.** You will learn the symbols easily as you progress through the book. A pronunciation key of the different consonants of American English with their IPA and dictionary symbols is presented on page 8. Refer to it often for a quick review.

To help you learn the exact pronunciation of the phonetic symbols and key words, the **Key to Pronouncing the Consonants of American English** on the next page has been recorded at the beginning of Tape 1, Side A. Each phonetic symbol will be pronounced and each English key word will be said twice. Listen carefully to this first recording **before** continuing with the program.

DEFINITIONS

As you progress through this manual, you will frequently see the terms **gum ridge, soft palate, aspiration, voiced consonant, voiceless consonant,** and **articulators**. We will now define these terms for you.

A KEY TO PRONOUNCING THE CONSONANTS OF AMERICAN ENGLISH

International Phonetic Alphabet Symbol	Dictionary Symbol	English Key Words	Spanish Key Words*
[s]	s	sit, basket, kiss	sí, cine, zapato
[z]	z	zoo, busy, buzz	mismo, isla, desde
[t]	t	top, return, cat	tiempo, tengo, siete
[d]	d	day, ladder, bed	mundo, mandar, decir
[θ]	th	think, bathtub, mouth	
[ð]	th	the, father, smooth	lado, nada, modo
[ʃ]	sh	shoe, nation, wish	
[tʃ]	ch	chair, witch	chico, ocho, muchacho
[ʒ]	zh	rouge, vision, measure	
[dʒ]	j	jaw, magic, age	
[j]	y	you, yes	vaya, pollo, hielo
[p]	p	pay, apple, stop	poco, papel, esperar
[b]	b	boy, rabbit, tub	tambor, también
[f]	f	fun, office, if	feliz, enfermo, frío
[v]	v	very, over, save	
[k]	k	cake, car, book	como, casa, kilo
[g]	g	go, begin, egg	tengo, gato, guerra
[w]	w	we, away	huele, hueso, guarder
[l]	l	lamp, pillow, bell	linda, calma, falso
[r]	r	red, marry, car	
[h]	h	hat, behind	jugar, mujer, gente
[m]	m	me, swim	mama, comer
[n]	n	no, run	una, nada, mano
[ŋ]	ŋ	sing, playing	tengo, banco

*Spanish key words contain consonants that are close approximations for the American English target sound. They are not always technically equal examples.

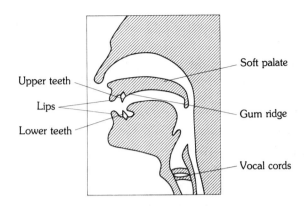

Upper teeth

Lips

Lower teeth

Soft palate

Gum ridge

Vocal cords

GUM RIDGE: The gum ridge is the hard part of the roof of your mouth which is just behind your upper front teeth.

SOFT PALATE: The soft palate is the soft, movable, rear portion of the roof of your mouth.

ASPIRATION: Aspiration means the action of pronouncing a sound with a puff of released breath. Certain consonants in English ([p], [t], [k], and [h]) are "aspirate" sounds. They should be produced with a strong puff of air.

VOICED CONSONANT: A voiced consonant is a sound produced when the vocal cords are vibrating. Place your hand on your throat over your vocal cords while making a humming sound. You can feel your vocal cords vibrate as you say "*mmmmmmmmm.*"

VOICELESS CONSONANT: A voiceless consonant is a sound made with no vibration of the vocal cords. Put your hand over your vocal cords and make the hissing sound "*ssssssss.*" You will *not* feel any vibration this time!

ARTICULATORS: The articulators are the different parts of the mouth area that we use when speaking, such as the lips, tongue, soft palate, teeth, and jaw.

The various consonant sounds are created by:

1. **The position of your articulators.** For example, the tip of your tongue must touch the upper gum ridge to say sounds like [t], [d], [n], or [l] but must protrude between your teeth to say [θ] as in think or [ð] as in them.

2. **The way the airstream comes from your mouth or nose.** For example, the air or breath stream is continuous for the consonants [s] or [f] but is completely stopped and then exploded for [p] or [t]. The airstream

flows through the <u>nose</u> for [m], [n], and [ŋ] and through the <u>mouth</u> for all other consonants.

3. **The vibration of your vocal cords.** For example, your vocal cords do <u>not</u> vibrate for the sounds [s], [f], or [t], but you must add "voicing" for the sounds [z], [v], or [d].

The following chart categorizes the voiced and voiceless consonants. Don't try to memorize the chart! Put your hand over your vocal cords as you say the following sounds. You will be able to hear *and* ***"feel"*** the difference between voiced and voiceless consonants.

VOICED	VOICELESS
[b]	[p]
[d]	[t]
[g]	[k]
[v]	[f]
[z]	[s]
[ð]	[θ]
[dʒ]	[tʃ]
[ʒ]	[ʃ]
[m], [n], [ŋ]	[h]
[j], [w], [l], [r]	

```
****************************************************
```

[s] as in *SIT, BASKET,* and *KISS*
⟨DICTIONARY MARK: *S*⟩
AND
[z] as in *ZOO, BUSY,* and *BUZZ*
⟨DICTIONARY MARK: *Z*⟩

```
****************************************************
```

PRONOUNCING [s]

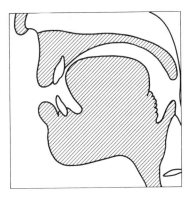

TIP OF TONGUE:	**is near but does not touch gum ridge behind upper front teeth.***
AIRSTREAM:	**is continuous without interruption.**
VOCAL CORDS:	**are not vibrating.**

The sound [s] is pronounced in the same way as the Spanish letters s̲ and z̲.

SPANISH KEY WORDS WITH [s]

Spanish words with this sound may be spelled with s̲, z̲, or c̲.

 KEY WORDS: *s̲i* *s̲iete* *z̲apato* *c̲ine*

POSSIBLE PRONUNCIATION PROBLEMS
FOR THE SPANISH SPEAKER

The sound [s] is a common sound in Spanish and should be easy for you to say. However, in Spanish the vowel e̲ comes before [s] in many words: escuela, estudiante, espanol. Thus you might incorrectly say e̲ before [s] in English.

*Some speakers produce [s] more easily by placing the tip of the tongue behind the lower front teeth.

EXAMPLES: If you produce e before [s]:   **state** will sound like **estate**
say   will sound like **essay**
steam will sound like **esteem**

As you say [s], keep the airstream steady, like the *hissing* sound of a snake (*sssssssss*)! Remember, in Spanish it's *escuela* and *estudiar*, but in English it's **school** and **study. SO STUDY and PRACTICE; you'll SOON have SUCCESS with** [s]!

 **EXERCISE A**

The following words should be pronounced with [s]. Repeat them after your teacher or the instructor on the tape. (Do not begin any [s] words with the vowel e.)

[s] **At the Beginning**	[s] **In the Middle**	[s] **At the End**
sky	lesson	bus
sad	racing	yes
spin	listen	box
slow	pencil	miss
skip	custom	face
spell	basket	makes
study	answer	house
snake	castle	course
skate	history	class
school	fast	plus

[s] **Spelled**

"*s*"	"*c*"	"*x*" ([ks])	"*ss*"
spy	cell	six	kiss
ski	ice	fix	less
smoke	lace	fox	dresser
steak	cent	tax	message
desk	center	oxen	

Less frequent spelling patterns for [s] consist of the letters z and sc.

EXAMPLES: waltz   pretzel   scent   scene

> **HINTS:** 1. The letter <u>s</u> is the most common spelling pattern for [s].
>
> 2. The letter <u>c</u> followed by <u>e</u>, <u>i</u>, or <u>y</u> is usually pronounced [s].
>
>   EXAMPLES: <u>c</u>ent pla<u>c</u>e so<u>c</u>iety fan<u>cy</u>
>
> 3. The letter <u>s</u> in plural nouns is pronounced [s] when it follows most voiceless consonants.
>
>   EXAMPLES: book<u>s</u> coat<u>s</u> cuff<u>s</u> map<u>s</u>

EXERCISE B

The boldface words in the following phrases and sentences should be pronounced with [s]. Read them aloud as accurately as possible. (Avoid using the vowel <u>e</u> before [s].) **This exercise is not on the tape.**

1. **stop sign**
2. **small mistake**
3. **start** and **stop**
4. **Nice** to **see** you!
5. **stand straight**
6. **sit still!**

7. **Speak** for **yourself**.
8. The **swimmer** was **slow** and **steady**.
9. The **store started selling cigarettes**.
10. **Stan stopped smoking**.
11. We had **steak** and **spinach** for **supper**.
12. **Students study** in **school**.
13. I **rest** on **Saturday** and **Sunday**.
14. The **sportsman likes** to **ski** and **skate**.
15. **Stacy speaks Spanish**.

 SELF-TEST I (Correct answers may be found in the Appendix on p. 190.)

Listen carefully to your teacher or to the tape as the following 10 words are presented. Some of them will be deliberately mispronounced. Circle **C** for "Correct" or **I** for "Incorrect" to indicate if the word was pronounced correctly or incorrectly.

EXAMPLE A: seven C (I) (The instructor says **"eseven."**)

EXAMPLE B: Spain (C) I (The instructor says **"Spain."**)

1.	school	C	I	6.	study	C	I
2.	start	C	I	7.	slow	C	I
3.	student	C	I	8.	skating	C	I
4.	snake	C	I	9.	salad	C	I
5.	smoking	C	I	10.	stealing	C	I

PRONOUNCING [z]

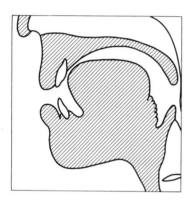

TONGUE:	**is in the same position as for [s].**
AIRSTREAM:	**is continuous without interruption.**
VOCAL CORDS:	**are vibrating.**

In many dialects of Spanish, the letter s followed by a voiced consonant (m, l, d, g) is pronounced like [z].

EXAMPLES: *mismo   isla   desde   rasgar*

POSSIBLE PRONUNCIATION PROBLEMS FOR THE SPANISH SPEAKER

The sound [z] is not a common sound in Spanish. You probably pronounce the letter z in English the same way as you would in Spanish (like [s]). Also, irregular English spelling patterns contribute to your problems with this consonant.

EXAMPLES: If you say [s] instead of [z]: **zoo** will sound like **Sue**

eyes will sound like **ice**

prize will sound like **price**

Remember, [z] is a voiced sound; your vocal cords MUST vibrate or you will say [s] by mistake. ***Think of the "buzzing" sound of a bee (bZZZZZZZZZ) and you'll say your Z's with EASE!***

EXERCISE A

The following words should be pronounced with [z]. Repeat them after your teacher or the instructor on the tape. (Be sure to add voice by making your vocal cords vibrate.)

[z] **At the Beginning**	[z] **In the Middle**	[z] **At the End**
zoo	lazy	as
zeal	busy	is
zest	easy	his
zinc	crazy	was
zero	razor	buzz
zone	dozen	daze
zebra	dizzy	raise
zipper	cousin	amaze
	puzzle	breeze

[z] **Spelled:**

"*z*"	"*s*"
zip	has
size	eyes
seize	rose
lizard	these
sneeze	bruise

The letter x is a less common spelling pattern for [z].

EXAMPLES: xylophone xerox

HINTS: 1. The letter z is usually pronounced [z].

        EXAMPLES: zipper cozy freeze

      2. The letter s is usually pronounced [z] when between vowels in a stressed syllable.

        EXAMPLES: desérve becáuse resígn presént

      3. The letter s in plural nouns is pronounced [z] when it follows a vowel or most voiced consonants.

        EXAMPLES: shoes legs leaves beds cars

NOTE: The vowel BEFORE [z] at the end of a word is always prolonged more than before [s]. Prolonging the vowel before [z] helps to distinguish it from [s].*

      EXAMPLES: eyes breeze rise buzz

EXERCISE B

The boldface words in the following phrases and sentences should be pronounced with [z]. Repeat them carefully after your teacher or the instructor on the tape. (Remember to add voicing when saying words with [z].)

1. **Easy does** it.
2. **zero degrees**
3. a cool **breeze**
4. a **dozen eggs**
5. **busy as** a bee
6. **Close** your **eyes**.

7. The **puzzle is easy**.
8. I **raise flowers**.
9. There are **zebras** and **lions** at the **zoo**.
10. **His cousin comes** from New **Zealand**.
11. The **museum is closed** on **Tuesday**.
12. My **husband** gave me a **dozen roses**.
13. I'm **crazy** about **raisins** and **apples**.
14. **Liza** took a **cruise** to **Brazil**.
15. The **jazz music is pleasant**.

*The same rule applies to the voiced consonants [b], [d], [v], and [g]. (See appropriate chapters.)

 **SELF-TEST I** (Correct answers may be found in the Appendix on p. 190.)

Repeat the following words after your teacher or the Instructor on the tape. Circle the letter s in each word that is pronounced [z]. **(Only ONE s in each word is actually pronounced [z].)**

EXAMPLE: surpri(s)e

1. suppose
2. Susan
3. disaster
4. easiest
5. tissues

6. salesman
7. season
8. resist
9. presents
10. business

 **SELF-TEST II** (Correct answers may be found in the Appendix on p. 190.)

Listen carefully to your teacher or the tape as each four-word series is presented. Circle the **ONE** word in each group that is **NOT** pronounced with [z].

EXAMPLE: is   was   his   (this)

1.	eyes	nose	wrist	ears
2.	walls	waltz	wells	ways
3.	carrots	apples	peas	raisins
4.	pleasing	pleasant	pleasure	please
5.	deserve	daisy	serve	design
6.	cease	seize	size	sings
7.	Tuesday	Thursday	Wednesday	Saturday
8.	east	ease	easy	tease
9.	rose	rice	raise	rise
10.	fox	xylophone	clothes	zero

```
*******************************************
```
CONTRAST AND REVIEW OF [s] and [z]
```
*******************************************
```

 ## ORAL EXERCISE I

Repeat the pairs of words and sentences carefully after your teacher or the instructor on the tape. **REMEMBER**, [z] is a voiced sound; your vocal cords should vibrate. (Be sure to prolong any vowel BEFORE the sound [z].)

[s]	[z]
1. **S**ue	**z**oo
2. fa**ce**	pha**se**
3. ra**ce**	rai**se**
4. bu**s**	bu**zz**
5. i**ce**	eye**s**

6. We saw the **place**.   We saw the **plays**.
7. They made **peace**.   They made **peas**.
8. The **price** was $100.   The **prize** was $100.
9. Did you see the **racer**?   Did you see the **razor**?
10. He lost the **race**.   He lost the **raise**.

11. **Sue** went to the **zoo**.
      [s]   [z]
12. Put **ice** on your **eyes**.
        [s]   [z]
13. My **niece** hurt her **knees**.
         [s]   [z]
14. The **president** set a **precedent**.
        [z]   [s]
15. The baby will **lose** his **loose** tooth.
          [z]   [s]

[s] VS. [z] IN NOUN/VERB PAIRS

Several nouns and verbs are the same in the written form. However, we can distinguish between these word pairs in their spoken form. The letter s in the noun is pronounced [s]; in the verb it is pronounced [z].

 ## ORAL EXERCISE II

Repeat the following words and sentences after your teacher or the instructor on the tape. Be sure to add "voice" to the letter s when saying the verbs.

Nouns		**Verbs**	
s = [s]		*s* = [z]	
1. excuse	(excusa)	excuse	(perdonar)
2. house	(casa)	house	(hospedarse)
3. use	(uso)	use	(usar; utilizar)
4. grease	(grasa)	grease	(lubricar; engrasar)
5. abuse	(abuso; mal uso)	abuse	(abusar de; injuriar)

6. Please **excuse** me.
    [z]   [z]

7. He has a good **excuse**.
    [z]   [s]

8. May I **use** your car?
    [z]

9. The object has no **use**.
        [z]   [s]

10. The museum will **house** the painting.
        [z]   [z]

11. We bought a new **house**.
            [s]

12. Child **abuse** is a terrible thing.
      [s]

13. Please don't **abuse** me.
    [z]   [z]

 **SELF-TEST I** (Correct answers may be found in the Appendix on p. 191.)

Listen carefully to your teacher or the tape as 10 three-word series are presented. Two of the words in each group will be the SAME; one will be DIFFERENT. Circle the number of the word that is **different**.

EXAMPLE: The instructor says: *prize price price*

You circle: ① 2 3

1. 1 2 3   6. 1 2 3
2. 1 2 3   7. 1 2 3
3. 1 2 3   8. 1 2 3
4. 1 2 3   9. 1 2 3
5. 1 2 3   10. 1 2 3

SELF-TEST II (Correct answers may be found in the Appendix on p. 191.)

Read the following sentences aloud. In the brackets provided above each boldface word, write the phonetic symbol ([s] or [z]) representing the sound of the underlined letters. **This self-test is not on the tape**.

EXAMPLE:
          [s]   [s] [z]
Silence is golden.

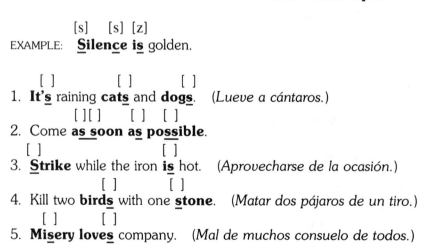

      [ ]   [ ]   [ ]
1. **It's** raining **cats** and **dogs**.   (*Lueve a cántaros.*)
          [ ][ ]   [ ]   [ ]
2. Come **as soon as possible**.
      [ ]   [ ]
3. **Strike** while the iron **is** hot.   (*Aprovecharse de la ocasión.*)
                [ ]   [ ]
4. Kill two **birds** with one **stone**.   (*Matar dos pájaros de un tiro.*)
      [ ]   [ ]
5. **Misery loves** company.   (*Mal de muchos consuelo de todos.*)

SELF-TEST III

(Correct answers may be found in the Appendix on p. 191.)

Your teacher or instructor on the tape will present the following sentences using ONLY ONE of the choices. Listen carefully and circle the word (and consonant) used.

EXAMPLE: The sweater was	(fussy [s]	**fuzzy).** **[z]**
1. We finally won the	(race [s]	raise). [z]
2. I know that	(face [s]	phase). [z]
3. He gave me a good	(price [s]	prize). [z]
4. Look at her small	(niece [s]	knees). [z]
5. We must accept the	(loss [s]	laws). [z]
6. The sheep have	(fleece [s]	fleas). [z]
7. Did you hear the	(bus [s]	buzz)? [z]
8. His dog has a large	(muscle [s]	muzzle). [z]
9. How much is the	(sink [s]	zinc)? [z]
10. I can identify the	(spice [s]	spies). [z]

SELF-TEST IV

(Correct answers may be found in the Appendix on p. 192.)

Read the following limericks aloud. Circle all words pronounced with [s] and underline all words pronounced with [z]. **This self-test is not on the tape.**

A Man Named (Stu)

A man from Texas named Stu
Was crazy about Silly Sue.
    He proposed twenty times,
      Using song, dance, and rhymes
Until Sue said to Stu, ''I do!''

A Girl Named Maxine

There was a slim girl called Maxine
She loved cooking Spanish cuisine
    She spent days eating rice,
      Lots of chickens and spice
Now Maxine is no longer lean!

LIMERICKS by L. R. Poms

FOR AN ENCORE . . .

Reading

Read several advertisements in your local newspaper. Underline all words pronounced with [s]; circle all [z] words. Practice reading the ad aloud. Be sure to pronounce the [s] and [z] words correctly.

```
*************************************************
```

[t] as in *TOP, RETURN,* and *CAT*
⟨DICTIONARY MARK: *t*⟩

```
*************************************************
```

PRONOUNCING [t]

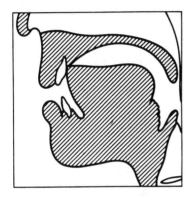

TONGUE TIP: is firmly pressed against gum ridge behind upper front teeth.

AIRSTREAM: is stopped and then exploded.

VOCAL CORDS: are not vibrating.

The sound [t] in English is similar to the sound of the Spanish letter *t*. (English [t] is aspirate and produced with a strong puff of air.)

SPANISH KEY WORDS WITH [t]

Spanish words with this sound are spelled with *t*.

KEY WORDS: *tiempo*   *tengo*   *siete*

POSSIBLE PRONUNCIATION PROBLEMS FOR THE SPANISH SPEAKER

The sound [t] is a familiar consonant for you. However, [t] is much more explosive in English than in Spanish. When speaking English, your tongue tip should touch the upper gum ridge and **NOT** the back of your upper front teeth. [t] must be said with strong aspiration and a puff of air* or it might sound like [d].

*When *t* is between two vowels and follows a stressed syllable (as in *water, butter, city,* etc.), it is NOT aspirated. *t* between vowels sounds like the Spanish *r* in such words as *caro, pero,* and *moro.*

When *t* follows *s* (as in *stop, stay, stick,* etc.), it is **NOT aspirated with a puff of air.

Practice saying [t] by loosely holding a tissue in front of your mouth. If you aspirate [t] correctly and say it with a puff of air, your tissue will flutter. *So—be sure to practice all the time; you'll make a terrific [t]!*

EXERCISE A

The following words should be pronounced with [t]. Repeat them after your teacher or the instructor on the tape.

[t] **At the Beginning**	[t] **In the Middle**	[t] **At the End**
to	until	it
ten	after	but
try	empty	ate
top	wanted	boat
talk	attend	went
tell	return	late
tree	winter	light
time	between	state
table	contain	fruit
terrible	printing	apart

> **HINTS:** 1. The letter *t* is usually pronounced [t].
>
> 2. The letters *ed* in past tense verbs are pronounced [t] when they follow a voiceless consonant.
>
> EXAMPLES: stopped looked kissed washed

EXERCISE B

Read the following words aloud. Remember, **the _t_ between vowels is usually NOT aspirated.** Pronounce it like the Spanish _r_ in _cara_ or _pero_. **This exercise is not on the tape.**

city	water
pretty	writing
better	sitting
notice	pattern
butter	cutting

EXERCISE C

Read the following phrases and sentences aloud. ***Be sure to say any t at the beginning of the boldface words with a puff of air.*** (Your tongue tip should be against your upper gum ridge and NOT the back of your teeth.) **This exercise is not on the tape.**

1. **Tell** the **teacher**.
2. **tea** and **toast**
3. **take apart**
4. **Take** your **time**.
5. **Today** is **Tuesday**.
6. **Turn** off the **light**.
7. **Tom bought two tickets.**
8. **Ten** and **ten** is **twenty**.
9. **Ted** has a **terrible temper**.
10. **Turn left at tenth street.**

Read the following words aloud. Circle the letter *t* in each word that is pronounced [t]. (Only **ONE** *t* in each word is actually pronounced [t]). **This self-test is not on the tape.**

EXAMPLE: t h o u g h(t)

1. t r a c t i o n
2. t h a t
3. p a t i e n t
4. t e x t u r e
5. t e m p e r a t u r e

6. t o o t h
7. p r e s e n t a t i o n
8. a r i t h m e t i c
9. t o g e t h e r
10. s u b t r a c t i o n

SELF-TEST II (Correct answers may be found in the Appendix on p. 193.)

Read the following sentences aloud. Circle the [t] word that correctly completes each sentence. Be sure to say [t] with a puff of air. **This self-test is not on the tape.**

1. (two   too)   **Tess** had _____ much **to eat.**
2. (two   too)   I **must return** _____ books.
3. (right   write)   "**Two** wrongs **don't** make a _____."
4. (right   write)   Please _____ me a **note.**
5. (aunt   ant)   **Tim's** _____ is **twenty-two.**

SELF-TEST III (Correct answers may be found in the Appendix on p. 193.)

Read the following dialogue aloud. Circle all words pronounced with [t]. **This self-test is not on the tape.**

. . . .

TOM: (Teresa,) who were you (talking) (to) on the telephone?
TERESA: Terry White. She wanted to know what time the party is tonight.
TOM: Terry is always late. She missed the tennis tournament last Tuesday.

TERESA:	Two days ago, she came to breakfast at two instead of ten A.M.
TOM:	Terry missed her flight to Texas last week.
TERESA:	She's never on time for any appointment.
TOM:	This is terrible! What time did you tell her to come tonight?
TERESA:	Don't worry. I had a terrific idea. I told Terry to come at six fifteen. The party really is set for eight!
TOM:	To tell the truth, I wish you told her it was at two fifteen. I just don't trust her!

. . . .

After checking your answers in the Appendix, practice the dialogue again with a friend. Remember to aspirate [t].

FOR AN ENCORE . . .

Conversation

Use the following common [t] phrases when talking to different people at home, school, or work: **What time is it? Take your time, What is your telephone number?**

⟨⟨EVERY TIME YOU TALK, TRY TO SAY A PERFECT [t]⟩⟩

```
************************************************
```

[d] as in *DAY, LADDER,* and *BED*
⟨DICTIONARY MARK: *d*⟩

```
************************************************
```

PRONOUNCING [d]

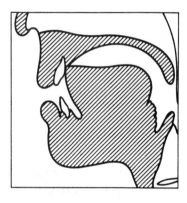

TONGUE TIP: is firmly pressed against gum ridge behind upper front teeth.

AIRSTREAM: is stopped and then exploded.

VOCAL CORDS: are vibrating.

The sound [d] in English is similar to the sound of the letter *d* when it begins a word or follows *n* or *l* in Spanish.

SPANISH KEY WORDS WITH [d]

Spanish words have this sound when *d* begins a word or follows *n* or *l*.

    KEY WORDS: *mun<u>d</u>o*   *man<u>d</u>ar*   *al<u>d</u>ea*   *<u>d</u>ecir*

POSSIBLE PRONUNCIATION PROBLEMS FOR THE SPANISH SPEAKER

1. The sound [d] should be produced with the tip of your tongue touching the upper gum ridge and **NOT** the back of your upper front teeth or placed between your teeth as in many Spanish words. If you don't touch the upper gum ridge when saying [d], it will contribute to your accent. It might even sound like [ð].

EXAMPLES: If you say [ð] instead of [d]:   ***ladder***   will sound like ***lather***
                                                    breeding will sound like ***breathing***

2. When [d] is the last sound in a word, many Spanish speakers forget to make their vocal cords vibrate. This will make [d] sound like a [t] and confuse your listeners.

EXAMPLES: If you say [t] instead of [d]: ***card*** will sound like ***cart***
bed will sound like ***bet***

Your [d] will be perfect if you press the tip of your tongue against the gum ridge behind your upper front teeth *and* add voicing. ***Don't forget to practice*** [d] ***every day!***

EXERCISE A

The following words should be pronounced with [d]. Repeat them after your teacher or the instructor on the tape. (Be sure your tongue tip touches the upper gum ridge.)

[d] **At the Beginning**	[d] **In the Middle**	[d] **At the End**
do	body	bad
dog	soda	did
day	under	end
desk	today	said
door	older	food
dime	order	card
down	window	cold
dozen	pudding	bread
doctor	Sunday	build
different	medicine	would

EXERCISE B

Read the following pairs of words aloud. Be sure to press your tongue tip against the upper gum ridge and to make your vocal cords vibrate for [d]. (Remember to prolong any vowel BEFORE the consonant [d].) **This exercise is not on the tape.**

[d]	[t]
bed	bet
mad	mat
need	neat
hard	heart
bride	bright
hide	height
wade	wait

EXERCISE C

Read the following phrases and sentences aloud. The boldface words should be pronounced with [d]. **This exercise is not on the tape.**

1. a **good idea**
2. one **hundred dollars**
3. **end** of the **road**
4. a **bad cold**
5. What's **today's date**?
6. How **do** you **do**?

7. What **did** you **order** for **dinner**?
8. **Wendy** is a **wonderful dancer**.
9. We **landed** in **London** at **dawn**.
10. **Send dad** a **birthday card**.

 **SELF-TEST I** (Correct answers may be found in the Appendix on p. 193.)

Listen carefully to your teacher or the tape as five sentences are presented. Some words that should be pronounced with [d] will be said INCORRECTLY. Circle **C** for "Correct" or **I** for "Incorrect" to indicate whether the [d] word in each sentence is properly pronounced.

Sentence	Response	
EXAMPLE A	Ⓒ I	(I'm reading a **good** book.)
EXAMPLE B	C Ⓘ	(**Sat** is the opposite of happy.)

1. C I
2. C I
3. C I
4. C I
5. C I

SELF-TEST II (Correct answers may be found in the Appendix on p. 194.)

Read the following wedding invitation aloud. Circle all words pronounced with [d]. **This self-test is not on the tape.**

Mr. and Mrs. Andrew Douglas
cordially invite you
to the wedding of their daughter
WENDY DOUGLAS
to
PEDRO DIAZ
on Sunday, the twenty-third of December,
at the Diner's Club
1020 Davis Road, Providence, Rhode Island

RECEPTION AND DINNER FOLLOWING WEDDING
RSVP by Wednesday, December third

FOR AN ENCORE . . .

Conversation

Start a conversation with such expressions as *"Today's a nice day, isn't it?"* or *"What's today's date; I don't remember?"*

⟪**DON'T FORGET TO PRACTICE [d] EVERY DAY!**⟫

```
*************************************************
```

[θ] as in *THINK, BATHTUB, and MOUTH*
⟨DICTIONARY MARK: *th*⟩

```
*************************************************
```

PRONOUNCING [θ]

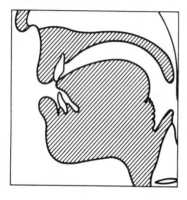

TONGUE TIP: is placed between the teeth.

AIRSTREAM: is continuous without interruption.

VOCAL CORDS: are not vibrating.

The sound [θ] is similar to the "Castillian lisp" used by *Madrilenos* when pronouncing such words as *hace* and *zapato*. (The letters *c* and *z* are produced with the tongue between the teeth.)

POSSIBLE PRONUNCIATION PROBLEMS FOR THE SPANISH SPEAKER

The sound [θ] does not exist in most dialects of Spanish. Because it may be difficult for you to recognize, you probably substitute more familiar sounds.

EXAMPLES: If you substitute [s] for [θ]:   ***thank*** will sound like ***sank***
                                            thing will sound like ***sing***

If you substitute [t] for [θ]:   ***path*** will sound like ***pat***

The sound [θ] will be easy for you to pronounce if you CONCENTRATE on placing your tongue between your teeth (***LOOK IN A MIRROR***), and keep the airstream continuous. From now on, you'll be able to say ***Thank you*** instead of ***sank you! KEEP THINKING ABOUT*** [θ]!

EXERCISE A

The following words should be pronounced with [θ]. Repeat them after your teacher or the instructor on the tape. (Remember to place your tongue between your teeth.)

[θ] **At the Beginning**	[θ] **In the Middle**	[θ] **At the End**
thaw	author	path
thin	wealthy	bath
thank	nothing	both
thief	healthy	cloth
theme	something	mouth
thick	anything	north
thorn	method	health
theory	Athens	teeth
thirsty	birthday	truth
thought	toothpaste	month

 ## EXERCISE B

Repeat the following pairs of words after your teacher or the instructor on the tape. Place your tongue **BETWEEN** your teeth for [θ] and **BEHIND** your teeth for [t] and [s].

I		II	
[θ]	[t]	[θ]	[s]
thank	tank	thank	sank
thin	tin	thin	sin
thought	taught	think	sink
bath	bat	bath	bass*
both	boat	thick	sick

*Bass = róbalo.

The boldface words in the following phrases and sentences should be pronounced with the consonant [θ]. Repeat them carefully after your teacher or the instructor on the tape.

1. **Thank** you.
2. I **think** so.
3. **something** else
4. Open your **mouth**.
5. **healthy** and **wealthy**
6. penny for your **thoughts**

7. **Thanksgiving** falls on **Thursday**.
8. Do birds fly **north** or **south** in the winter?
9. **Thank** you for your **thoughtful birthday** card.
10. The baby got his **third tooth** this **month**.
11. **Thelma** had her **thirty-third birthday**.
12. Brush your **teeth** with a **tooth**brush and **tooth**paste!
13. Good friends stick with you **through thick** and **thin**!*
14. The **author's theme** is **thought** provoking.
15. The **oath** is "Tell the **truth**, the whole **truth**, and **nothing** but the **truth**."

 **SELF-TEST I**   (Correct answers may be found in the Appendix on p. 194.)

Repeat the following words after your teacher or the instructor on the tape. (Only 10 of them are pronounced with [θ].) Circle the words pronounced with the [θ] sound.

Thomas	clothes	teeth	feather
Ruth	further	moth	father
although	thick	other	faith
throw	clothing	breathe	breath
rather	method	cloth	thorough

*Through thick and thin = *contra viento y marea.*

 **SELF-TEST II** (Correct answers may be found in the Appendix on p. 194.)

Listen carefully to your teacher or the tape as 10 words pronounced with [θ] are presented. Indicate where you hear the [θ] sound in each word by circling **Beginning**, **Middle**, or **End**.

EXAMPLES: A. The instructor says: ***think***

You circle: (Beginning) Middle End

B. The instructor says: ***north***

You circle: Beginning Middle (End)

1. Beginning Middle End
2. Beginning Middle End
3. Beginning Middle End
4. Beginning Middle End
5. Beginning Middle End
6. Beginning Middle End
7. Beginning Middle End
8. Beginning Middle End
9. Beginning Middle End
10. Beginning Middle End

SELF-TEST III (Correct answers may be found in the Appendix on p. 195.)

Read the following paragraph about ***Jim Thorpe*** aloud. Circle all words that should be pronounced with the consonant [θ]. **This self-test is not on the tape.**

· ·

Do you know (anything) about Jim (Thorpe?) He was an American Indian athlete. He excelled in everything at the Olympics. Thousands were angry when Thorpe's medals were taken away because he was called a professional athlete. In 1973, long after his death, Thorpe's medals were restored. Throughout the world, Jim Thorpe is thought to be one of the greatest male athletes.

· ·

After checking your answers in the Appendix, practice reading the paragraph again. Be sure to place your tongue BETWEEN your teeth as you say [θ].

FOR AN ENCORE . . .

Conversation

No one ever tires of hearing **Thank you!** Each time you say *thank you* to someone, be sure to pronounce the [θ] correctly.

⟨⟨**KEEP THINKING ABOUT** [θ]!⟩⟩

```
***********************************************
```

[ð] as in *THE, FATHER,* and *SMOOTH*
⟨DICTIONARY MARK: *th*⟩

```
***********************************************
```

PRONOUNCING [ð]

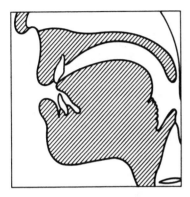

TONGUE TIP: is placed between the teeth.

AIRSTREAM: is continuous without interruption.

VOCAL CORDS: are vibrating.

The sound [ð] in English is similar to the sound of the letter *d* between vowels in certain Spanish words. ([ð] is actually stronger and more visible between the teeth.)

SPANISH KEY WORDS WITH [ð]

Spanish words have this sound when *d* is between two vowels.

KEY WORDS: *estados unidos   lado   nada   modo*

POSSIBLE PRONUNCIATION PROBLEMS FOR THE SPANISH SPEAKER

The sound [ð] doesn't exist at the beginning or end of words in Spanish. It may be difficult for you to recognize and produce. You probably substitute the more familiar [d] sound.

EXAMPLES: If you substitute [d] for [ð]:   ***they***   will sound like ***day***
lather   will sound like ***ladder***
breathe will sound like ***breed***

When pronouncing [ð], remember to place your tongue between your teeth and to keep the airstream from your mouth continuous. ***LOOK IN THE MIRROR* as you practice the [ð] exercises.** Make sure you can **SEE** the tip of your tongue, and such words as ***these, them***, and ***those*** will be pronounced perfectly!

 ## EXERCISE A

The following words should be pronounced with [ð]. Repeat them after your teacher or the instructor on the tape. (Be sure that your vocal cords are vibrating **AND** that your tongue is between your teeth.)

[ð] **At the Beginning**	[ð] **In the Middle**	[ð] **At the End**
the	other	bathe
this	mother	clothe
then	father	smooth
them	brother	breathe
that	gather	soothe
they	either	
those	neither	
there	leather	
these	together	
though		

HINT: The letters *th* followed by *e* are usually pronounced [ð].

EXAMPLES: the   them   other   bathe

EXERCISE B

Repeat the following pairs of words after your teacher or the instructor on the tape. Place your tongue **BETWEEN** your teeth for [ð] and **BEHIND** your teeth for [d].

[ð]	[d]
they	day
then	den
than	Dan
there	dare
though	dough
bathe	bade
lather	ladder
worthy	wordy
breathe	breed

EXERCISE C

The boldface words in the following phrases and sentences should be pronounced with the consonant [ð]. Repeat them carefully after your teacher or the instructor on the tape.

1. **That's** right.
2. **father** and **mother**
3. **either** one of **them**
4. **This** is it!
5. wet **weather**
6. Don't **bother** me!

7. **This** is my **other brother**.
8. I'd **rather** get **together another** day.
9. **That leather** belt feels **smooth**.
10. I like **this** one better **than the other** one.
11. **Mother** must **bathe the** baby.
12. Will **grandmother** and **grandfather** be **there**?
13. **This** bad **weather bothers father**.
14. **This clothing** is as light as a **feather**.
15. **The rhythm** of **the** music is **soothing**.

Listen carefully to your teacher or to the tape as 10 words pronounced with [ð] are presented. Indicate where you hear the [ð] sound in each word by circling **BEGINNING**, **MIDDLE**, or **END**.

EXAMPLES: a. The instructor says: *that*

You circle: (Beginning) Middle   End

b. The instructor says: *weather*

You circle: Beginning (Middle) End

1. Beginning   Middle   End
2. Beginning   Middle   End
3. Beginning   Middle   End
4. Beginning   Middle   End
5. Beginning   Middle   End

6. Beginning   Middle   End
7. Beginning   Middle   End
8. Beginning   Middle   End
9. Beginning   Middle   End
10. Beginning   Middle   End

SELF-TEST II   (Correct answers may be found in the Appendix on p. 195.)

Read the following sentences aloud. Circle the word that correctly completes the sentence. Be sure to place your tongue **BETWEEN** your teeth when pronouncing [ð]. **This self-test is not on the tape.**

1. (This   These) _____ shoes are **weatherproof**.
2. (weather   whether) I **loathe this** wet _____.
3. (This   These) _____ board is **smoother than the other** one.
4. (there   their) **The** family will be _____ for **the** wedding.
5. (they   them) **Mother** told _____ not to be late.
6. (They   Them) _____ are **worthy** of **the** award.
7. (Those   That) _____ **brothers** are **rather** tall.
8. (weather   whether) I don't know _____ to buy **this** one or **that** one.
9. (That   Those) _____ **lather** is **soothing**.
10. (Their   there) _____ **father** likes **the weather** in **southern** Florida.

Read the following dialogue aloud. Circle all words that should be pronounced with the consonant [ð]. **This self-test is not on the tape.**

. . . .

(The) Photo Album

DAUGHTER: (Mother,) I like (these) old pictures. Who's (this?)

MOTHER: That's your great grandmother.

DAUGHTER: The feathered hat is funny! Who's that man?

MOTHER: That's your grandfather. He was from the Netherlands.

DAUGHTER: I know these people! Aren't they Uncle Tom and Uncle Bob?

MOTHER: That's right. Those are my brothers. They always bothered me!

DAUGHTER: This must be either father or his brother.

MOTHER: Neither! That's your father's uncle.

DAUGHTER: Why are there other people in this photo?

MOTHER: This was a family gathering. We got together all the time.

DAUGHTER: Mother, who's this "smooth"-looking man?

MOTHER: Shhhhhhhhh! I'd rather not say. Your father will hear!

DAUGHTER: Is that your old boyfriend?

MOTHER: Well, even mothers had fun in those days!

. . . .

After checking your answers in the Appendix, practice the dialogue again. Try it with a friend; be sure to feel your tongue between your teeth as you say the [ð] words.

FOR AN ENCORE . . .

Reading

Select a brief newspaper or magazine article. Circle all words pronounced with the consonant [ð]. Look in a mirror as you read it aloud. Be sure to see and feel the tip of your tongue between your teeth as you say [ð].

REVIEW

[s] [z] [t] [d] [θ] [ð]

[s]

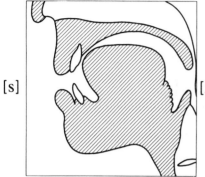

[z]

[s] **ENGLISH KEY WORDS:** *Sue   bus   ice*
[z] **ENGLISH KEY WORDS:** *zoo   buzz   eyes*

The tongue is near but does NOT touch the upper gum ridge. The airstream is continuous. The vocal cords DON'T vibrate for [s]; they DO vibrate for [z].

[s] **SPANISH KEY WORDS:** *si   siete   cine*
[z] **SPANISH KEY WORDS:** *mismo   desde   isla*

[t]

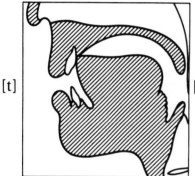

[d]

[t] **ENGLISH KEY WORDS:** *to   ten   coat*
[d] **ENGLISH KEY WORDS:** *do   den   code*

The tongue tip is firmly pressed against the upper gum ridge. The airstream is stopped and then exploded. The vocal cords DON'T vibrate for [t]; they DO vibrate for [d].

[t] **SPANISH KEY WORDS:** *tiempo   tengo   siete*
[d] **SPANISH KEY WORDS:** *mundo   aldea   decir*

[θ]

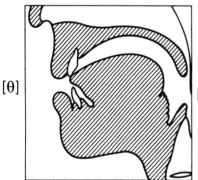

[ð]

[θ] **ENGLISH KEY WORDS:** *think   method   bath*
[ð] **ENGLISH KEY WORDS:** *the   father   smooth*

The tongue tip is placed between the teeth. The airstream is continuous. The vocal cords DON'T vibrate for [θ]; they DO vibrate for [ð].

[θ] **SPANISH KEY WORDS:** — — —
[ð] **SPANISH KEY WORDS:** *lado   nada   modo*

REVIEW EXERCISE

Repeat the rows of words and sentences after your teacher or the instructor on the tape.

[θ]	[t]	[s]	[z]
1. **th**ick	**t**ick	**s**ick	
2. **th**ank	**t**ank	**s**ank	
3. **th**rough	**tw**o	**S**ue	**z**oo
4. fai**th**	fa**t**e	fa**ce**	pha**se**
5. my**th**	mi**tt**	mi**ss**	M**s**.

[ð]	[d]	[t]
6. **th**en	**d**en	**t**en
7. **th**ough	**d**ough	**t**oe
8. ba**the**	ba**de**	bai**t**
9. wri**the**	ri**de**	wri**te**
10. **th**ere	**d**are	**t**ear

11. It's a good **faith**. It's a good **fate**. It's a good **face**. It's a good **phase**.
       [θ]   [t]   [s]   [z]

12. I went to **Beth**. I went to **bet**. I went to **Bess**. I went to **bed**.
       [θ]   [t]   [s]   [d]

13. The **raid** is set. The **rate** is set. The **race** is set. The **raise** is set.
       [d]   [t]   [s]   [z]

14. She began to **ride**. She began to **write**. She began to **writhe**. She began to **rise**.
       [d]   [t]   [ð]   [z]

15. Don't **dip** it. Don't **tip** it. Don't **sip** it. Don't **zip** it.
       [d]   [t]   [s]   [z]

16. **Dan** is older **than Stan**.
    [d]   [ð]   [s]

17. Did you **pass Pat** on the **path**.
              [s] [t]   [θ]

18. I **think** there is **zinc** in the **sink**.
       [θ]   [z]   [s]

19. **Seth said** to **set** the table.
       [θ]   [d]   [t]

20. **Sue** is **due** at the **zoo** at **two**.
    [s]   [d]   [z]   [t]

REVIEW TEST I

(Correct answers may be found in the Appendix on p. 196.)

Read the following words aloud carefully. On the lines above each word write the number of the phonetic symbol representing the sound of the underlined letters. **This review test is not on the tape.**

Pronunciation Key:
1 = [s] as in **sit**   4 = [d] as in **dog**
2 = [z] as in **zoo**   5 = [θ] as in **think**
3 = [t] as in **to**   6 = [ð] as in **them**

EXAMPLE:
<u>3 5 1</u>
too<u>th</u>pa<u>s</u>te

1. <u>th</u>ou<u>s</u>and

2. <u>s</u>ou<u>th</u>we<u>s</u>t

3. <u>th</u>e<u>s</u>e

4. a<u>th</u>le<u>t</u>e

5. bir<u>th</u>day car<u>d</u>

After checking your answers in the Appendix, use each of the words in a sentence. Be sure to pronounce all consonant sounds carefully.

REVIEW TEST II

(Correct answers may be found in the Appendix on p. 197.)

Read each four-word series aloud. Circle the **ONE** word in each group of four pronounced with a consonant different from the other words. On the line to the left, write the number and corresponding phonetic symbol for the sound common to the other three words. **This review test is not on the tape.**

Pronunciation Key:
1 = [s] as in **sit**   4 = [d] as in **dog**
2 = [z] as in **zoo**   5 = [θ] as in **think**
3 = [t] as in **to**   6 = [ð] as in **them**

EXAMPLE:	6	[ð] brother	breathe	(breath)	breathing
1.	[ ] think	through	thought	another
2.	[ ] rice	rise	raisin	phase
3.	[ ] duck	soldier	deep	fed
4.	[ ] weather	cloth	their	bathe
5.	[ ] Tim	Terry	Thomas	Beth

REVIEW TEST III
(Correct answers may be found in the Appendix on p. 197.)

Your teacher or instructor on the tape will present the following sentences using only **ONE** of the words in parentheses. Listen carefully and circle the word (and consonant) used.

EXAMPLE: The ((sum   thumb) is very big.
                    [s]   [θ]

1. Did you make the   (bed   bet)?
                              [d]   [t]

2. The doctors didn't use   (either   ether).
                              [ð]   [θ]

3. Steven doesn't like to miss (math   Mass).
                                [θ]   [s]

4. It is a   (worthy   wordy) article.
                              [ð]   [d]

5. I like to   (raise   race)   horses.
                              [z]   [s]

6. Please give him the   (time   dime).
                              [t]   [d]

7. They announced the   (truth   truce).
                              [θ]   [s]

8. (Teasing   teething) makes the baby cry.
    [z]   [ð]

9. The boy doesn't want to   (think   sink).
                              [θ]   [s]

10. Before you know it,   (they   day)   will be here.
                              [ð]   [d]

After checking your answers in the Appendix, read each of the sentences twice. Carefully pronounce the first word in parenthesis in the first reading and the contrast word in the second reading.

REVIEW TEST IV

(Correct answers may be found in the Appendix on p. 198.)

Read the following selections aloud **SLOWLY!** On the line above each word, write the number of the phonetic symbol that represents the sound of the underlined letters. **This review test is not on the tape.**

Pronunciation Key:

1 = [s] as in **sit**   4 = [d] as in **dog**
2 = [z] as in **zoo**   5 = [θ] as in **think**
3 = [t] as in **to**   6 = [ð] as in **then**


```
  3  1 1
```
Let Us Smile

The thing that goes the farthest,

  towards making life worthwhile,

That costs the least, and does the most,

  is just a pleasant smile!

It's full of worth and goodness too,

  with manly kindness blent,

It's worth a million dollars,

  and it doesn't cost a cent!

(by Wilbur D. Nesbit)

```
****************************************************
```

[ʃ] as in *SHOE, NATION,* and *WISH*

⟨DICTIONARY MARK: *sh*⟩

AND

[tʃ] as in *CHAIR, TEACHER,* and *WITCH*

⟨DICTIONARY MARK: *ch*⟩

```
****************************************************
```

PRONOUNCING [ʃ]

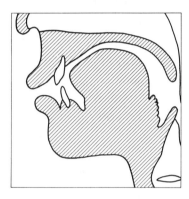

TIP OF TONGUE:	near but does not touch upper gum ridge.
MIDDLE OF TONGUE:	near but does not touch hard palate.
AIRSTREAM:	is continuous without interruption.
VOCAL CORDS:	are not vibrating.

POSSIBLE PRONUNCIATION PROBLEMS FOR THE SPANISH SPEAKER

The consonant [ʃ] does not exist in Spanish. You probably substitute the more familiar [tʃ] sound (the sound to be covered in the next section).

EXAMPLES: If you substitute [tʃ] for [ʃ]:   ***shoe*** will sound like ***chew***
wash will sound like ***watch***

The sound [ʃ] will be easy to pronounce if you keep the airstream steady and smooth. Be careful not to let your tongue touch your teeth or upper gum ridge or you will say [tʃ] by mistake. [ʃ] is a steady, QUIET sound. *Shhhhhhhh!*

 **EXERCISE A**

The following words should be pronounced with [ʃ]. Repeat them after your teacher or the instructor on the tape. (Remember: Don't let your tongue touch the roof of your mouth!)

[ʃ] **At the Beginning**	[ʃ] **In the Middle**	[ʃ] **At the End**
shy	ocean	dish
shop	washer	wish
ship	tissue	cash
shine	insure	wash
shoe	nation	rush
short	patient	finish
share	mission	punish
sugar	official	foolish
shape	machine	Spanish
shower	brushing	English

[ʃ] **Spelled**

"sh"	*"ti"*	*"ci"*	*"ss"*	*"ch"*
shelf	option	social	issue	chef
shirt	section	special	assure	chute
brush	fiction	musician	depression	machine
crash	mention	physician	profession	Chicago
shadow	election	conscious	expression	chauffeur

Less frequent spelling patterns for [ʃ] consist of the letters *s*, *ce*, and *xi*.

EXAMPLES: <u>s</u>ugar pen<u>s</u>ion o<u>c</u>ean an<u>x</u>ious

> *HINTS:* 1. The most common spelling pattern for [ʃ] consists of the letters *sh*.
>
> 2. The letters *t*, *ss*, and *c* before suffixes beginning with *i* are usually pronounced [ʃ].
>
> EXAMPLES: na<u>t</u>ion profe<u>ss</u>ion so<u>c</u>ial

 **EXERCISE B**

The boldface words in the following phrases and sentences should be pronounced with the [ʃ] sound. Repeat them carefully after your teacher or the instructor on the tape.

1. **Shake** hands.
2. **washing machine**
3. I'm **sure**!
4. **short** on **cash**
5. **Shut** the door!
6. **Polish** your **shoes**.

7. There are many **fish** in the **ocean**.
8. **Shirley shopped** for **shoes**.
9. The **shirt should** be **washed**.
10. The **mushrooms** and **shrimp** are **delicious**.
11. We had a **short vacation** in **Washington**.
12. **Shine** the **flashlight** in this **direction**.
13. **She showed** us the **chic** new **fashions**.
14. **Charlotte** speaks **English** and **Spanish**.
15. I **wish** you would **finish washing** the **dishes**.

 SELF-TEST I   (Correct answers may be found in the Appendix on p. 198.)

Listen carefully to your teacher or the tape as each four-word series is presented. Circle the ONE word in each group of four that is NOT pronounced with [ʃ].

EXAMPLE:	(pleasure)	sure	surely	sugar
1.	crush	cash	catch	crash
2.	chef	chief	chute	chiffon
3.	machine	parachute	mustache	kitchen
4.	China	Russia	Chicago	Michigan
5.	musician	physician	chemist	electrician
6.	pressure	pressed	assure	permission
7.	division	subtraction	addition	multiplication
8.	position	action	patio	motion
9.	Charlotte	Cheryl	Sharon	Charles
10.	tension	resign	pension	mention

PRONOUNCING [tʃ]

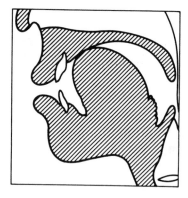

TONGUE TIP: is firmly pressed against gum ridge behind upper front teeth.

AIRSTREAM: is stopped (as for [t]) and then released (as for [ʃ]).

VOCAL CORDS: are not vibrating.

The sound [tʃ] is similar to the sound of the Spanish letters *ch*. It begins as the consonant [t] and ends as the consonant [ʃ].

SPANISH KEY WORDS WITH [tʃ]

Spanish words with this sound are spelled with *ch*.

     KEY WORDS: *chico*   *ocho*   *muchacho*   *cha cha cha*

POSSIBLE PRONUNCIATION PROBLEMS FOR THE SPANISH SPEAKER

Although [tʃ] is a familiar sound in Spanish, it is easy to confuse with the similar English sound [ʃ].

EXAMPLES: If you say [ʃ] instead of [tʃ]:   ***chair*** will sound like ***share***
                                                 which will sound like ***wish***

Just remember to start [tʃ] with your tongue in the same place as for the sound [t]. Be sure to press your tongue tip against the gum ridge behind your upper front teeth, or you will say [ʃ] by mistake. [tʃ] is an explosive sound— like a sneeze! Think of ***Ah-CHOO*** and you'll get [tʃ] just right! ***MEET THE CHALLENGE of*** [tʃ]!

 **EXERCISE A**

The following words should be pronounced with [tʃ]. Repeat them after your teacher or the instructor on the tape. (Be sure to begin [tʃ] just like the sound [t].)

[tʃ] **At the Beginning**	[tʃ] **In the Middle**	[tʃ] **At the End**
chew	nature	itch
chair	teacher	each
child	picture	match
chalk	hatchet	much
chest	butcher	reach
choose	richer	touch
cherry	orchard	watch
chicken	question	speech
Charles		sandwich
cheerful		

[tʃ] **Spelled**

"ch"	*"tu"*	*"tch"*
chop	mature	patch
rich	culture	catch
cheap	posture	butcher
cheese	fortune	kitchen
march	picture	pitcher

Less frequent spelling patterns for [tʃ] consist of the letters *t* and *ti*.

EXAMPLES: righteous   digestion   question

HINT: The most common spelling pattern for [tʃ] consists of the letters *ch*.

 **EXERCISE B**

The boldface words in the following phrases and sentences should be pronounced with the consonant [tʃ]. Repeat them carefully after your teacher or the instructor on the tape. (It's important that you remember to press your tongue tip against your upper gum ridge.)

1. **Watch** out!
2. **inch** by **inch**
3. I'm **catching** a cold.
4. **cheese sandwich**
5. Don't **touch** that!
6. **chocolate chip** cookies

7. The **chocolate chip** cookies are in the **kitchen**.
8. Does the **butcher charge much** for **chickens**?
9. **Which furniture** did you **choose**?
10. **Natural cheddar cheese** is not **cheap**.
11. Please **watch** the **children** in the **lunch**room.
12. I **purchased** a **picture** of **China**.
13. The **coach chose Charles** for the team.
14. The **bachelor** plays **checkers** and **chess**.
15. Don't count your **chickens** before they're **hatched**!*

---

*Count your chickens before they're hatched = vender la piel del oso antes de cazarlo.

52 [ʃ] as in SHOE and [tʃ] as in CHAIR

 **SELF-TEST I** (Correct answers may be found in the Appendix on p. 198.)

Listen carefully as your teacher or the instructor on the tape presents 10 sentences. Some words that should be pronounced with [tʃ] will be said INCORRECTLY. Circle **C** for **"Correct"** or **I** for **"Incorrect"** to indicate whether the [tʃ] word in each sentence is pronounced properly.

SENTENCE   **RESPONSE**

EXAMPLE A   C (I) (Sit in the **share**.)

EXAMPLE B   (C) I (I had to **change** a tire.)

1.   C I
2.   C I
3.   C I
4.   C I
5.   C I
6.   C I
7.   C I
8.   C I
9.   C I
10.   C I

****

CONTRAST AND REVIEW
OF [ʃ] AND [tʃ]

****

 **ORAL EXERCISE**

Repeat the pairs of words and sentences carefully after your teacher or the instructor on the tape. **REMEMBER**, your tongue tip must touch the upper gum ridge for [tʃ] but NOT for [ʃ].

[ʃ]   [tʃ]

1. **sh**oe   **ch**ew
2. **sh**are   **ch**air
3. **sh**ip   **ch**ip
4. wa**sh**   wat**ch**
5. ca**sh**   cat**ch**

6. I have a **crush**.   I have a **crutch**.
7. Please **wash** the dog.   Please **watch** the dog.
8. He can't **mash** it.   He can't **match** it.
9. Give me my **share**.   Give me my **chair**.
10. Get rid of the **sheet**!   Get rid of the **cheat**!

11. Let's **choose** new **shoes**.
       [tʃ]   [ʃ]
12. **She's** eating the **cheese**.
       [ʃ]   [tʃ]
13. **Sherry** likes **cherry** pie.
       [ʃ]   [tʃ]
14. The hull of the **ship** has a **chip**.
                          [ʃ]   [tʃ]
15. He paid **cash** for the **catch** of the day.
                    [ʃ]   [tʃ]

SELF-TEST I   (Correct answers may be found in the Appendix on p. 199.)

Listen carefully to your teacher or the instructor on the tape as 10 three-word series are presented. Two of the words in each series will be the SAME; one will be DIFFERENT. Circle the number of the word that is DIFFERENT.

EXAMPLE: The instructor says: *watch   watch   wash*

You circle: 1   2   ③

1. 1 2 3   6. 1 2 3
2. 1 2 3   7. 1 2 3
3. 1 2 3   8. 1 2 3
4. 1 2 3   9. 1 2 3
5. 1 2 3   10. 1 2 3

SELF-TEST II   (Correct answers may be found in the Appendix on p. 199.)

Read each of the following sentences aloud. In the brackets provided above each boldface word, write the phonetic symbol ([ʃ] or [tʃ]) representing the consonant in that word. **This self-test is not on the tape.**

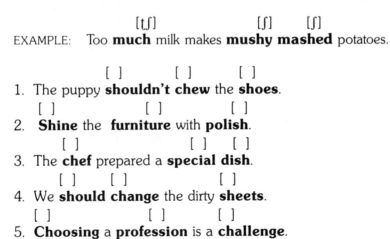

          [tʃ]   [ʃ]   [ʃ]
EXAMPLE: Too **much** milk makes **mushy mashed** potatoes.

           [ ]   [ ]   [ ]
1. The puppy **shouldn't chew** the **shoes**.
      [ ]   [ ]   [ ]
2. **Shine** the **furniture** with **polish**.
        [ ]   [ ] [ ]
3. The **chef** prepared a **special dish**.
        [ ]   [ ]   [ ]
4. We **should change** the dirty **sheets**.
      [ ]   [ ]   [ ]
5. **Choosing** a **profession** is a **challenge**.

SELF-TEST III (Correct answers may be found in the Appendix on p. 199.)

Your teacher or the instructor on the tape will present the following sentences using **ONLY ONE** of the choices. Listen carefully and circle the word (and consonant) used.

EXAMPLE: You sure can   (shop   chop).
                                 [ʃ]   [tʃ]

1. I didn't see the   (dish   ditch).
                              [ʃ]   [tʃ]

2. He hurt his   (shin   chin).
                              [ʃ]   [tʃ]

3. Did you hear that   (shatter   chatter)?
                              [ʃ]   [tʃ]

4. It's a silly   (wish   witch).
                              [ʃ]   [tʃ]

5. It was an endless   (marsh   march).
                              [ʃ]   [tʃ]

6. She brought me the   (wash   watch).
                              [ʃ]   [tʃ]

7. They have a large   (share   chair).
                              [ʃ]   [tʃ]

8. We must fix the   (ship   chip).
                              [ʃ]   [tʃ]

9. Does she have a new   (crush   crutch)?
                              [ʃ]   [tʃ]

10. They completed the   (shore   chore).
                              [ʃ]   [tʃ]

After checking your answers in the Appendix, read each of the sentences twice. Use the first word in the first reading and the contrast word in the second reading.

SELF-TEST IV

(Correct answers may be found in the Appendix on p. 200.)

Read the following dialogue aloud. CIRCLE all words pronounced with [ʃ] and UNDERLINE all words with [tʃ]. **This self-test is not on the tape.**

. . . .

CHAVO: Hi, Marshall. Do you have any change for the washing machine?

MARSHALL: Chavo, what are you doing washing clothes?

CHAVO: My wife, Sharon, is visiting family in Michigan. I'm watching the children.

MARSHALL: Watch out! Don't put bleach on those shirts. You'll wash out the color.

CHAVO: Will you teach me how to wash clothes?

MARSHALL: Be sure to wash white shirts separately. Don't use too much soap.

CHAVO: I wish Sharon would return. It's more natural for a woman to wash and shop.

MARSHALL: You sound like a chauvinist!* I don't mind doing chores. I'm great in the kitchen, too!

CHAVO: Would you like to take charge? I'll cheerfully pay you cash!

MARSHALL: Listen old chap—I'm a bachelor and too old to chase after children. I'm in a rush. It's been nice chatting with you, Chavo.

CHAVO: Sure—nice chatting with you too, Marshall.

. . . .

After checking your answers in the Appendix, practice the dialogue aloud with a friend.

*Chauvinist = chauvinista.

```
***********************************************
```

[ʒ] as in *MEASURE, VISION,* and *ROUGE*
⟨DICTIONARY MARK: *zh*⟩

```
***********************************************
```

PRONOUNCING [ʒ]

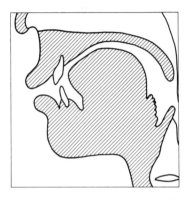

TONGUE:	**is in the same position as for [ʃ].**
AIRSTREAM:	**is continuous without interruption.**
VOCAL CORDS:	**are vibrating.**

The [ʒ] sound exists in the Spanish of Argentina, Uruguay, and central Colombia. In these countries, the Spanish letters *y* and *ll* are pronounced [ʒ] in such words as *yo* and *llamar.*

POSSIBLE PRONUNCIATION PROBLEMS FOR THE SPANISH SPEAKER

The sound [ʒ] does not exist in most dialects of Spanish. Your pronunciation problems occur because of similarities between [ʃ] and [ʒ].

EXAMPLES: If you substitute [ʃ] for [ʒ]:   ***vision*** will sound like "***vishion***"
beige will sound like "***beish***"

Be sure your vocal cords are vibrating when you say [ʒ] or you will substitute [ʃ] instead. (***Put your hand on your throat; FEEL THE VIBRATION!***) *It will be a **pleasure** to pronounce* [ʒ]!

EXERCISE A

The following words should be pronounced with [ʒ]. Repeat them accurately after your teacher or the instructor on the tape. (In English, [ʒ] does not occur at the beginning of words.)

[ʒ] **In the Middle**	[ʒ] **At the End**
Asia	rouge
usual	beige
vision	mirage
leisure	garage
measure	corsage
pleasure	massage
occasion	prestige
decision	camouflage
division	
television	

[ʒ] **Spelled:**

"si"	*"su"*	*"gi"* or *"ge"*
lesion	closure	beige
vision	unusual	regime
explosion	casual	massage
conclusion	composure	negligee
collision		camouflage
illusion		

A less frequent spelling pattern for [ʒ] consists of the letters *zu*.

EXAMPLES: a**zu**re   sei**zu**re

EXERCISE B

The boldface words in the following phrases and sentences should be pronounced with [ʒ]. Repeat them carefully after your teacher or the instructor on the tape.

1. color **television**
2. long **division**
3. That's **unusual**!
4. big **decision**
5. What's the **occasion**?
6. It's a **pleasure** to meet you.

7. A **mirage** is an **illusion**.
8. The **azure** skies are **unusual**.
9. She bought a **beige negligee**.
10. We **usually** watch **television**.
11. Get a **massage** at your **leisure**.
12. The **excursion** was a **pleasure**.
13. I heard an **explosion** in the **garage**.
14. The **collision** caused great **confusion**.
15. She received a **corsage** for the **occasion**.

SELF-TEST I

(Correct answers may be found in the Appendix on p. 200.)

Listen carefully to your teacher or to the tape as each four-word series is presented. Circle the ONE word in each group of four that is not pronounced with [ʒ].

EXAMPLE:	composure	exposure	enclosure	(position)
1.	leisure	pleasure	sure	measure
2.	Asia	Asian	Parisian	Paris
3.	huge	beige	rouge	prestige
4.	passion	collision	occasion	decision
5.	massage	mirage	message	corsage
6.	confusion	conclusive	contusion	conclusion
7.	lesion	profession	explosion	aversion
8.	vision	version	television	visible
9.	seizure	seize	azure	division
10.	treasury	treasurer	treason	treasure

Read each of the following sentences aloud. In the brackets provided above each boldface word, write the phonetic symbol ([ʒ] or [ʃ]) representing the consonant sound in that word. (Refer back to the chapter on [ʃ] as necessary.) **This self-test is not on the tape**.

[ʃ]   [ʒ]
EXAMPLE: We will **vacation** in **Asia.**

[ ]   [ ]
1. The **commission** made a **decision**.
            [ ]   [ ]
2. The class learned **division** and **addition**.
   [ ]   [ ]
3. **Measure** the **garage**.
      [ ]   [ ]
4. Your **profession** has **prestige**.
      [ ] [ ]   [ ]
5. That's an **unusual shade** of **rouge**.

SELF-TEST III   (Correct answers may be found in the Appendix on p. 201.)

Listen carefully to your teacher or to the tape as the following newscast is read. Circle all words pronounced with the [ʒ] sound.

Good evening. This is ⟨Frazier⟩ White with the 10:00 P.M. ⟨television⟩ news. Here are some ⟨unusual⟩ items.

**** Tourists on a pleasure trip discovered buried treasure. The treasure dates back to ancient Persia.

**** An explosion took place in a garage on First Avenue. Seizure of a bomb was made after much confusion.

**** Asian flu is spreading. Asian flu vaccinations will be available to those with exposure to the germ.

**** Today was the Parisian fashion show. Everything from casual leisure clothes to negligees was shown. Beige is the big color. Hemlines measure two inches below the knee.

In conclusion, carry your raincoat. Occasional showers are due tomorrow. Hope your evening is a pleasure. This is Frazier White saying GOOD NIGHT!

. . . .

After checking your answers in the Appendix, practice reading the broadcast aloud. (Pretend you are a famous newscaster!)

FOR AN ENCORE . . .

Reading

Read *TV Guide* or the television section of the newspaper aloud one evening to your family. Underline all [ʒ] words; be sure to pronounce them carefully.

REMEMBER, KEEP PRACTICING AND . . .

⟨⟨*IT WILL BE A PLEASURE TO PRONOUNCE* [ʒ]⟩⟩

```
*************************************************
```

[ʤ] as in *JAM, MAGIC,* and *AGE*
⟨DICTIONARY MARK: *j*⟩
AND
[j] as in *YOU* and *YES*
⟨DICTIONARY MARK: *y*⟩

```
*************************************************
```

PRONOUNCING [ʤ]

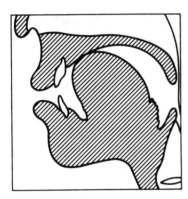

TONGUE TIP:		**is firmly pressed against gum ridge behind upper front teeth.**
AIRSTREAM:		**is stopped (as for [d]) and then released (as for [ʒ]).**
VOCAL CORDS:		**are vibrating.**

The sound [ʤ] exists in most dialects of Spanish when the letters *y* or *ll* begin the first word in a sentence. The use of [ʤ] is particularly evident in the Spanish of Chile, Paraguay, Puerto Rico, the Dominican Republic, and parts of Cuba and Bolivia.

SPANISH KEY WORDS WITH [ʤ]

Spanish words frequently have this sound when *y* or *ll* begin the first word in a sentence.

    KEY WORDS: *Yo no voy.*   *Llamo al medico.*

POSSIBLE PRONUNCIATION PROBLEMS
FOR THE SPANISH SPEAKER

Confusing English spelling patterns and similarities between [ʤ] and other sounds cause your pronunciation problems with [ʤ].

EXAMPLES: If you substitute [j] for [ʤ]: **_Jello_** will sound like **_yellow_**
If you substitute [h] for [ʤ]: **_jam_** will sound like **_ham_**
If you substitute [ʒ] for [ʤ]: **_large_** will sound like [lɑrʒ]

Just remember to start [ʤ] with your tongue in the same place as for the sound [d]. Be sure your tongue is pressed against your upper gum ridge AND that your vocal cords are vibrating when you say [ʤ]. **_JUST keep practicing!_** **_It will be a JOY to say_** [ʤ]!

EXERCISE A

The following words should be pronounced with [ʤ]. Repeat them after your teacher or the instructor on the tape. (Be sure to begin [ʤ] just like the sound [d].)

[ʤ] **At the Beginning**	[ʤ] **In the Middle**	[ʤ] **At the End**
jam	agent	age
joy	adjust	cage
job	magic	large
jar	enjoy	edge
gym	angel	badge
gem	injure	ridge
jail	danger	village
jello	suggest	marriage

[ʤ] **Spelled:**

_"j"_	**_"g"_**	**_"dg"_**
jaw	giant	fudge
joke	gentle	badge
June	ranger	budge
major	giraffe	wedge
subject	college	grudge

Less frequent spelling patterns for [ʤ] consist of the letters "_di_" and "_du_".

EXAMPLES: sol<u>di</u>er cor<u>di</u>al gra<u>du</u>ate e<u>du</u>cate

> **HINTS:** 1. The letter "*j*" is usually pronounced [dʒ].
>
> EXAMPLES: joke june January just John
>
> 2. The letter "*g*" before silent "*e*" at the end of a word is usually pronounced [dʒ].*
>
> EXAMPLES: age wedge village college

EXERCISE B

The boldface words in the following phrases and sentences should be pronounced with [dʒ]. Repeat them carefully after your teacher or the instructor on the tape.

1. **Just** a moment.
2. **Enjoy** yourself!
3. **pledge** of **allegiance**
4. Fourth of **July**
5. **college education**
6. **Jack** of all trades†
7. **Jim** is **just joking**.
8. **Jane enjoys jogging**.
9. The **major joined** the **legion**.
10. I **graduate** from **college** in **June**.
11. The **passengers** were **injured** in the **jeep**.
12. **John** mailed a **large package**.
13. Do you like **fudge**, **Jello**, or **gingerbread**?
14. The **engineer** lost his **job** in **January**.
15. The **agent** took a **jet** to **Japan**.

*Review exceptions to this hint on page 59, ([ʒ] At the End).

†*Jack of all trades = persona de muchas aptitudes.*

[dʒ] as in JAM and [j] as in YOU **65**

You're taking a jet around the world! Plan your itinerary by circling the countries pronounced with [ʤ]. **This exercise is not on the tape.**

(Java)	Guatemala	(Jerusalem)	Greece
England	Germany	Jamaica	Hungary
Japan	Greenland	Algeria	Egypt
Belgium	Argentina	China	Luxembourg

After checking your answers in the Appendix, practice the names of the countries by using them in the sentence *"**I'm taking a jet to** _____."*

SELF-TEST II (Correct answers may be found in the Appendix on p. 202.)

Listen carefully to your teacher or the tape as each 4-word series is presented. Circle the ONE word in each group of four that is *not* pronounced with [ʤ].

EXAMPLE:	gym	gypsy	jet	(guy)
1.	bulge	bug	budge	badge
2.	major	soldier	general	captain
3.	gentle	gem	intelligent	hen
4.	angel	angle	age	adjective
5.	jug	July	hug	juice
6.	giant	gin	gill*	giraffe
7.	educate	graduate	cordial	duck
8.	lung	lunge†	lounge	large
9.	Jill	Gene	Joan	Gary
10.	Germany	Greenland	Georgia	Virginia

*Gill = agalla.

† Lunge = arremetida.

PRONOUNCING [j]

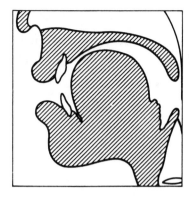

TONGUE: **is in the same position as for the vowel [i].**

AIRSTREAM: **is continuous without interruption.**

VOCAL CORDS: **are vibrating.**

The consonant [j] in English is similar to the sound of the letters *y*, *ll*, and *hie* in most dialects of Spanish.

SPANISH KEY WORDS WITH [j]

Spanish words with this sound are spelled with *y*, *ll*, or *hie*.

KEY WORDS: *va<u>y</u>a*   *po<u>ll</u>o*   *<u>hie</u>lo*   *<u>hie</u>rba*

POSSIBLE PRONUNCIATION PROBLEMS FOR THE SPANISH SPEAKER

In many dialects of Spanish, speakers vary in their use of the sounds [j] and [ʤ]. In English, these sounds cannot be used interchangeably without confusing your listeners!

EXAMPLES: If you say [ʤ] instead of [j]:   ***yet*** will sound like ***jet***
you will sound like ***Jew***

To pronounce [j] correctly, be sure the tip of your tongue is against the back of your lower front teeth and NOT touching the roof of your mouth. Remember the Spanish key words *pollo, vaya,* and *hierba* and ***YOU'LL* get *YOUR*** [j] ***sound YET***!

 **EXERCISE A**

The following words should be pronounced with [j]. Repeat them carefully after your teacher or the instructor on the tape. (In English, the consonant [j] does not occur at the end of words.)

[j] At the Beginning

yes
you
yell
use
year
yard
young
youth
yesterday

[j] In the Middle

onion
canyon
lawyer
beyond
values
regular
backyard
formula

[j] Spelled

"*y*"	"*i*"	"*u*"
yet	union	amuse
your	junior	music
yawn	senior	united
yolk	million	usual
yellow	familiar	university

> **HINTS:**
> 1. The most common spelling pattern for [j] is the letter "*y*" followed by a vowel.
>
>   EXAMPLES: y̲east y̲ou can̲y̲on farmy̲ard
>
> 2. When *y* is the first letter in a word, it is ALWAYS pronounced [j]; it is NEVER pronounced [ʤ].

NOTE: Distinguish between the vowel [u] and the consonant/vowel combination [ju].

[u]	[ju]
food	feud
booty	beauty
fool	fuel

Some English speakers add [j] after [n, t, d], or [s] in certain words: *news*, *Tuesday*, *duty*, *suit*. We will not practice that pronunciation of [j] in this manual.

EXERCISE B

The boldface words in the following phrases and sentences should be pronounced with the consonant [j]. Repeat them carefully after your teacher or the instructor on the tape. (Be sure you **DON'T** use [ʤ] by mistake!)

1. Nice to see **you**.
2. How are **you**?
3. **yes** or no?
4. Help **yourself**.
5. **You** look great!
6. in my **opinion**
7. Did **you** get **your** car fixed?
8. The **view** of the **canyon** is **beautiful**.
9. Did **you** eat **yams** or **yellow** rice?
10. **Your senior** class **reunion** is this **year**.
11. **You** shouldn't **yell** at **young** children.
12. **Your lawyer** is **brilliant**!
13. The New **York** City **mayor** was **young**.
14. Have **you** had some **yogurt yet**?
15. **Yesterday** we sailed on a **millionaire's yacht**.

Read each of the following sentences aloud. Complete the words appropriately. **This self-test is not on the tape**.

EXAMPLES: The **young** man proposed. She said **YES**.

1. The **youth** left. He hasn't come back **YE_**.
2. The player ran 50 **yards**. The crowds began to **YE__**.
3. Today is Monday. **YE_____** was Sunday.
4. Egg **yolks** should be **YE_____**.
5. **You** should get a check-up* once a **YE__**.

 SELF-TEST II (Correct answers may be found in the Appendix on p. 202.)

Listen carefully to your teacher or to the tape as 5 pairs of sentences are presented. Circle **SAME** if both sentences in each pair are the same. If they are NOT the same, circle **DIFFERENT**.

Pair	Response	
EXAMPLE A	ⓈAME DIFFERENT	(He is **young**. He is **young**.)
EXAMPLE B	SAME ⒹIFFERENT	(I heard **yes**. I heard **Jess**.)
1.	SAME DIFFERENT	
2.	SAME DIFFERENT	
3.	SAME DIFFERENT	
4.	SAME DIFFERENT	
5.	SAME DIFFERENT	

*Check-up = reconocimiento médico.

****

CONTRAST AND REVIEW OF [ʤ] and [j]

****

ORAL EXERCISE

Repeat the pairs of words and sentences carefully after your teacher or the instructor on the tape. **REMEMBER**, your tongue tip must touch the upper gum ridge for [ʤ] and touch the back of your lower front teeth for [j].

[ʤ]	[j]
1. jell	yell
2. Jello	yellow
3. joke	yolk
4. jeer*	year
5. major	mayor

6. Did they come by **jet**?   Did they come by **yet**?
7. It has no **juice**.   It has no **use**.
8. He became a **major**.   He became a **mayor**.
9. We went to **jail**.   We went to **Yale**.
10. The **jam** is sweet.   The **yam** is sweet.

11. Do **you** like **yellow Jello**?
    [j]   [j]   [ʤ]
12. **Jess** said **yes**.
    [ʤ]   [j]
13. Did the **jet** leave **yet**?
        [ʤ]   [j]
14. The crowds **jeered** this **year**.
           [ʤ]   [j]
15. **Jim** found a **jar** in his **yard**.
    [ʤ]   [ʤ]   [j]

*Jeer = burlarse.

SELF-TEST I
(Correct answers may be found in the Appendix on p. 203.)

Your teacher or the instructor on the tape will say only ONE word in each of the following pairs. Listen carefully and circle the word that you hear.

EXAMPLE: A. (jam) yam

            B.   Jess (yes)

1.   jet   yet
2.   joke   yolk
3.   jot†   yacht
4.   Jew   you
5.   juice   use

SELF-TEST II
(Correct answers may be found in the Appendix on p. 203.)

Listen carefully to your teacher or the tape as 10 sentences are presented. One word in each sentence will be said **INCORRECTLY**. On the line to the right of each number, write the **CORRECT** word for the sentence.

Sentence   **Correct Word**

EXAMPLE A   joke _____   (I heard a funny (**yolk**).)

EXAMPLE B   yell _____   (Please don't **jell** so loud!)

1.   _____
2.   _____
3.   _____
4.   _____
5.   _____
6.   _____
7.   _____
8.   _____
9.   _____
10.   _____

*Yak = yak; cotorrear.

† Jot = apunte; jota.

SELF-TEST III

(Correct answers may be found in the Appendix on p. 203.)

Read the following paragraph aloud. Circle all words pronounced with [ʤ] and underline all words that should be pronounced with [j]. **This self-test is not on the tape**.

Do you know what *YANKEE* means? People from the United States are generally called *Yankees*. Soldiers from the northern region were called *Yankees* during the Civil War. George M. Cohan wrote a stage hit called *Yankee Doodle Dandy*. Jealous baseball fans waged war over the New York Yankees and Dodgers for years. Whether you are from Georgia or New Jersey, you should enjoy being called a *Yank!*

FOR AN ENCORE . . .

Conversation

Remember to use such words as **YOU**, **YOUR**, and so on correctly in conversation. Practice such phrases as *"Nice to see YOU," "How are YOU," "Say hello to YOUR wife."*

The key to perfect pronunciation is *PRACTICE*   *PRACTICE*   *PRACTICE*.

《《*YOU'LL ENJOY SAYING* [ʤ] and [j]》》

*CONGRATULATIONS! **You've just completed the section with some of the most difficult consonants to say. To help perfect your pronunciation of** [ʃ], [tʃ], [ʒ], [ʤ], **and** [j], **we've prepared a series of review activities for you.***

```
*********************************************
```

REVIEW

[ʃ] [tʃ] [ʒ] [ʤ] [j]

```
*********************************************
```

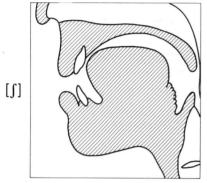

[ʃ]

ENGLISH KEY WORDS: *shoe   nation   wish*

The tongue is near but does NOT touch the roof of the mouth. The airstream is continuous but the vocal cords are NOT vibrating.

SPANISH KEY WORDS: — — —

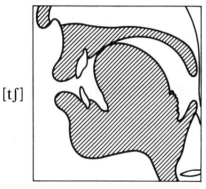

[tʃ]

ENGLISH KEY WORDS: *chair   teacher   witch*

The tongue tip is firmly pressed against the upper gum ridge. The airstream is stopped and then released with an explosion. The vocal cords are NOT vibrating.

SPANISH KEY WORDS: *chico   ocho   muchacho*

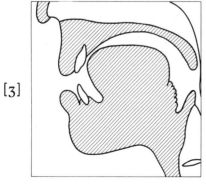

[ʒ]

ENGLISH KEY WORDS: *measure   vision   rouge*

The tongue is in the same position as for [ʃ]. The airstream is continuous AND the vocal cords ARE vibrating.

SPANISH KEY WORDS: — — —

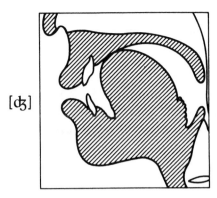

[ʤ]

ENGLISH KEY WORDS: *jaw   magic   age*

The tongue is in the same position as for [tʃ]. The airstream is stopped and then released with an explosion. The vocal cords ARE vibrating.

SPANISH KEY WORDS: — — —

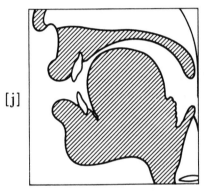

[j]

ENGLISH KEY WORDS: *you   yes*

The tongue is in the same position as for the [i] vowel. The airstream is continuous AND the vocal cords ARE vibrating.

SPANISH KEY WORDS: *vaya   pollo   hielo*

Your teacher or the instructor on the tape will present 10 three-word series. Write the number 1, 2, or 3 on the line above each word to correspond with the order of word presentation. **Listen carefully to the first consonant sound in each word.**

EXAMPLE: The instructor says: **sham   jam   yam**

You write: <u>3</u>   <u>1</u>   <u>2</u>
             yam sham jam

1. <u>   </u> cheer   <u>   </u> jeer   <u>   </u> year

2. <u>   </u> cheap   <u>   </u> jeep   <u>   </u> sheep

3. <u>   </u> chew   <u>   </u> shoe   <u>   </u> you

4. <u>   </u> cello   <u>   </u> Jello   <u>   </u> yellow

5. <u>   </u> choose   <u>   </u> shoes   <u>   </u> Jews

6. <u>   </u> chin   <u>   </u> shin   <u>   </u> gin

7. <u>   </u> choke   <u>   </u> joke   <u>   </u> yolk

8. <u>   </u> cherry   <u>   </u> Jerry   <u>   </u> Sherry

9. <u>   </u> your   <u>   </u> chore   <u>   </u> shore

10. <u>   </u> chose   <u>   </u> shows   <u>   </u> Joe's

REVIEW TEST II

(Correct answers may be found in the Appendix on p. 204.)

Pronounce the words in each of the following groups. Write the number and corresponding phonetic symbol for the sound common to each list of words at the top of the column. **This review test is not on the tape**.

Pronunciation Key:

1 = [ʃ] as in **shoe**
2 = [tʃ] as in **chair**
3 = [ʒ] as in **beige**

4 = [ʤ] as in **jam**
5 = [j] as in **you**

EXAMPLE: <u>1</u> [ʃ]
shop
shore
shout
show

1. ____ [ ]
onion
union
million
billion

2. ____ [ ]
chef
chute
chic
chiffon

3. ____ [ ]
nature
picture
capture
furniture

4. ____ [ ]
division
occasion
explosion
television

5. ____ [ ]
Russia
tissue
passion
mission

6. ____ [ ]
gradual
cordial
soldier
education

7. ____ [ ]
chief
catch
question
ketchup

8. ____ [ ]
cute
yawn
amuse
senior

9. ____ [ ]
ridge
angel
suggest
general

10. ____ [ ]
vision
rouge
garage
pleasure

After checking your answers in the Appendix, practice pronouncing the preceding words again.

Your teacher or instructor on the tape will present the following sentences using ONLY ONE of the choices. Listen carefully and circle the word (and consonant) used.

EXAMPLE: ((Chess   Jess) can be difficult.
            [tʃ]   [dʒ]

1. The (sheep   jeep) is very old.
         [ʃ]   [dʒ]
2. The (legion   lesion) is large.
         [dʒ]   [ʒ]
3. My friend (Sherry   Jerry) is nice.
              [ʃ]   [dʒ]
4. The (cash   catch) was counted.
         [ʃ]   [tʃ]
5. I don't like (Jello   yellow).
                 [dʒ]   [j]
6. The (mayor   major) made a speech.
         [j]   [dʒ]
7. The crowd (cheered   jeered) loudly.
               [tʃ]   [dʒ]
8. The (dishes   ditches) are dirty.
         [ʃ]   [tʃ]
9. The (badge   batch) was given out.
         [dʒ]   [tʃ]
10. Did you see the (etching   edging)?
                    [tʃ]   [dʒ]

After checking your answers in the Appendix, read each of the sentences twice. Use the first word in the first reading and the contrast word in the second reading.

REVIEW TEST IV

(Correct answers may be found in the Appendix on p. 205.)

Listen carefully to your teacher or to the tape as 10 groups of three words are presented. Circle the phonetic symbol that identifies the consonant sound each group of words has in common.

EXAMPLE: The instructor says: *chair   chop   cheap*

You circle: ([tʃ])   [ʃ]   [ʒ]

1. [tʃ]   [ʒ]   [ʤ]   6. [ʤ]   [j]   [tʃ]
2. [tʃ]   [ʃ]   [ʤ]   7. [ʤ]   [j]   [tʃ]
3. [tʃ]   [ʃ]   [ʤ]   8. [ʃ]   [ʒ]   [ʤ]
4. [tʃ]   [ʃ]   [ʤ]   9. [ʃ]   [ʒ]   [ʤ]
5. [ʤ]   [j]   [tʃ]   10. [ʃ]   [ʒ]   [ʤ]

REVIEW TEST V

(Correct answers may be found in the Appendix on p. 205.)

Read the following story about **George Washington** aloud. Find all the words pronounced with either [ʃ], [tʃ], [ʒ], [ʤ], or [j] and write them under the appropriate phonetic symbols. (Words containing two of the consonants should appear under two different columns) **This review test is not on the tape.**

. . . .

George Washington was the first president of the United States. He was a just man with much courage. His contributions can never be measured.

Washington was born in the year 1732 in Virginia. A legend about his boyhood shows his honesty. He chopped down a cherry tree but wouldn't lie to his father.

Washington was a general during the American Revolution. He showed unusual compassion to his soldiers at Valley Forge. He was in charge at the Constitutional Convention. Finally, he was elected as the first president of the United States. Washington was a commander-in-chief whose decisions helped make America a great nation. Past and future generations shall remember George Washington as the father of our country.

. . . .

[ʃ] **as in** *shoe*	[tʃ] as in *chair*	[ʒ] as in *beige*	[ʤ] as in *jam*	[j] as in *you*
Washington				

```
************************************************
```

[p] as in *PAY, APPLE,* and *STOP*
⟨DICTIONARY MARK: *p*⟩

```
************************************************
```

PRONOUNCING [p]

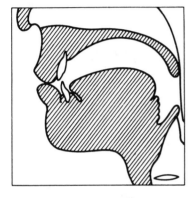

LIPS: **are pressed together.**

AIRSTREAM: **is stopped and then exploded.**

VOCAL CORDS: **are not vibrating.**

The sound [p] in English is similar to the sound of the letter *p* in Spanish.
(English [p] is more aspirate and is produced with a stronger puff of air.)

SPANISH KEY WORDS WITH [p]

Spanish words with this sound are spelled with *p*.

    KEY WORDS: *poco*   *papel*   *esperar*

POSSIBLE PRONUNCIATION PROBLEMS
FOR THE SPANISH SPEAKER

This is a familiar consonant to you. However, [p] is much more explosive in
English than it is in Spanish. When speaking English, [p] at the beginning of
words must be produced with strong aspiration and a puff of air* or it might
sound like [b].

EXAMPLES::   If you forget to aspirate [p]:   **pear** could sound like ***bear***
                                             pat   could sound like ***bat***

*When *p* follows *s* (as in *spot, spend, spy,* etc.), it is **NOT** aspirated with a puff of air.

Practice saying [p] by loosely holding a tissue in front of your lips. If you aspirate [p] correctly and say it with a puff of air, your tissue will flutter. *So PUFF, PUFF, PUFF, and you'll PRONOUNCE a PERFECT [p]!*

 ## EXERCISE A

The following words should be pronounced with [p]. Repeat them after your teacher or the instructor on the tape.

[p] **At the Beginning**	[p] **In the Middle**	[p] **At the End**
pen	open	top
put	apart	cap
pet	apple	lip
pay	happy	map
pig	pepper	stop
pot	paper	soap
pain	supper	pipe
past	airport	jump
person	people	camp

EXERCISE B

The boldface words in the following phrases and sentences should be pronounced with [p]. Read them aloud carefully. *Remember to aspirate [p] at the beginning of words!* **This exercise is not on the tape.**

1. **Stop** it!
2. **pencil** and **paper**
3. a **piece** of **pie**
4. **proud** as a **peacock**
5. **Open up**!
6. **Practice** makes **perfect**.

7. The **apples** and **pears** are **ripe**.
8. The **ship** will **stop** in **Panama**.
9. Wash the **pots** and **pans** with **soap**.
10. Her **purple pants** are **pretty**.

SELF-TEST I   (Correct answers may be found in the Appendix on p. 205.)

Read the following sentences aloud. Choose the correct word from the list to fill in the blanks. All answers contain the **NAME** of the letter **P**! **This self-test is not on the tape**.

peacock   peanuts   people   peeled   peach
Pete   peace   peeve   peak   P

1. A nickname for **Peter** is _____.
2. The **opposite** of war is _____.
3. **Pam** bought _____ to feed the elephants.
4. The **top** of a mountain is called a _____.
5. The **plural** of **person** is _____.
6. A **popular** fruit is a _____.
7. A bird with bright feathers is a _____.
8. **Potatoes** should be _____ before being cooked.
9. The letter **preceding** Q is _____.
10. Something that annoys you is called a "**pet** _____."

SELF-TEST II   (Correct answers may be found in the Appendix on p. 206.)

Read the following dialogue aloud. Circle all words pronounced with [p]. **This self-test is not on the tape**.

. . . .

The (Surprise) Trip

PABLO: Paulette, I have a surprise! We're taking a trip to Puerto Rico tonight!
PAULETTE: I'm very happy. But I need more time to prepare.
PABLO: That's simple. I'll help you pack.
PAULETTE: Who will care for our pet poodle?
PABLO: Your parents!
PAULETTE: Who will pick up the mail?
PABLO: Our neighbor Pete!
PAULETTE: Who will water the plants?

PABLO:	We'll put them on the patio.
PAULETTE:	Who will pay for the trip?
PABLO:	The company is paying every penny!
PAULETTE:	Pablo, you've really planned this.
PABLO:	Of course! I'm dependable, superior, and a perfect . . .
PAULETTE:	"Pain in the neck!"* Don't get carried away!

FOR AN ENCORE . . .

Reading

Practice the following tongue twister:

· ·

Peter Piper picked a peck of pickled peppers. How many pecks of pickled peppers did Peter Piper pick? A peck!

· ·

If you can master the **Peter Piper** tongue twister,† you can say [p] perfectly!

REMEMBER TO PUFF, PUFF, PUFF, AND

⟨⟨ *YOU'LL PRONOUNCE A PERFECT* [p]⟩⟩

Pain in the neck = chinche.
†*Tongue twister = trabalengua.*

```
*********************************************************
```

[b] as in *BOY, RABBIT,* and *TUB*
⟨DICTIONARY MARK: *b*⟩

```
*********************************************************
```

PRONOUNCING [b]

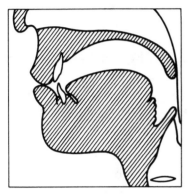

LIPS: are pressed together (as for [p]).

AIRSTREAM: is stopped and then exploded.

VOCAL CORDS: are vibrating.

The consonant [b] in English is similar to the sound of the letter *b* when it follows *n* or *m* or begins a sentence in Spanish.

SPANISH KEY WORDS WITH [b]

Spanish words have this sound when *b* follows *n* or *m* or begins a sentence.

KEY WORDS: *tam<u>b</u>ien*   *tam<u>b</u>or*   *<u>B</u>enito* tiene un *<u>b</u>uen <u>b</u>arco.*

POSSIBLE PRONUNCIATION PROBLEMS
FOR THE SPANISH SPEAKER

1. The Spanish letters *b* and *v* are frequently pronounced alike. You may confuse the two sounds in English.

   EXAMPLE: If you use [v] instead of [b]:   ***boat*** will sound like ***vote***

2. When [b] is the last sound in a word, many Spanish speakers forget to make their vocal cords vibrate. This will make [b] sound like [p] and confuse your listeners.

EXAMPLES:: If you say [p] instead of [b]: **robe** will sound like **rope**

cab will sound like **cap**

The consonant [b] will be easy to say if you make your vocal cords vibrate and firmly press your lips together. **BE sure to say** [b] **with a BOOM and you'll BE at your BEST!**

EXERCISE A

The following words should be pronounced with [b]. Repeat them after your teacher or the instructor on the tape.

[b] **At the Beginning**	[b] **In the Middle**	[b] **At the End**
be	obey	cab
but	baby	cub
bat	table	rub
back	habit	tub
best	rubber	rib
bone	lobby	rob
bank	cabin	knob
boat	label	crib
begin	ribbon	bulb
borrow	neighbor	robe

> **HINTS:** 1. The letter *b* is almost always pronounced [b]. (Note the exception described in the following hint.)
>
> 2. When *b* follows *m* in the same syllable, it is usually NOT pronounced.
>
> EXAMPLES: comb bomb lamb plumber

EXERCISE B

Repeat the following pairs of words after your teacher or the instructor on the tape. (Make certain that your lips are pressed together and that you add "voicing" when saying [b].)

[b]	[p]
robe	rope
mob	mop
tab	tap
rib	rip
stable	staple
symbol	simple

EXERCISE C

Read the following phrases and sentences aloud. Remember, the boldface words should be pronounced with the voiced consonant [b]. **This exercise is not on the tape**.

1. **bread** and **butter**
2. **above** and **below**
3. **baseball** game
4. **black** and **blue**
5. the **bigger** the **better**
6. I'll **be back**.

7. **Bad habits** can **be broken**.
8. **Bill** is in the **lobby**.
9. **Bob bought** a **blue bathrobe**.
10. **Betty** was **born** in **Boston**.

SELF-TEST I (Correct answers may be found in the Appendix on p. 206.)

Read the following sentences aloud. Circle the [b] word that correctly completes the sentence. Be sure to press your lips together when pronouncing [b]. **This self-test is not on the tape**.

1. (bread   bred)   I like rye _____.
2. (bear   bare)   Don't walk in your _____ feet.
3. (been   bin)   **Bob** has _____ here **before**.
4. (been   bin)   Please store the **beans** in the _____.
5. (blew   blue)   The wind _____ my **bag** away.
6. (blew   blue)   **Betty's** _____ **bonnet** is **becoming**.
7. (Buy   By)   _____ a **box** of **black buttons**.
8. (berry   bury)   The dog will _____ his **bone** in the **backyard**.

9. (bored   board)   My **brother** drinks **beer** when he's _____.
10. (bored   board)   The **builder** needs a **bigger** _____.

SELF-TEST II   (Correct answers may be found in the Appendix on p. 206.)

Read the following dialogue aloud. Circle all words pronounced with [b]. **This self-test is not on the tape.**

. . . .

BETTY: Benito, I bet you forgot my birthday!
BENITO: I bet I didn't. I bought you a birthday present.
BETTY: I can't believe it. What did you bring?
BENITO: It begins with the letter **B**.
BETTY: Oh, boy! It must be a bathrobe. You buy me one every birthday.
BENITO: It's not a bathrobe!
BETTY: Is it a bowling ball?
BENITO: No, it's not a bowling ball.
BETTY: It must be a book about boating, your favorite hobby.
BENITO: Betty, you're way off base.* I bought you a bracelet. A diamond bracelet!
BETTY: Wow! This is the best birthday present I ever got. You didn't rob a bank, did you?
BENITO: Don't worry. I didn't beg, borrow, or steal; just don't expect any more presents for a long time. I'm broke!†

FOR AN ENCORE . . .

Conversation

On your next three visits to a **boutique** or department store, be sure to tell the salesperson, "I'd like to **buy** a _____" (**black blouse**, **blue belt**, etc.) After each purchase, tell a friend or family member, "I **bought** a _____." Be sure to pronounce [b] correctly.

SAY [b] WITH A BOOM AND . . . .

⟨⟨*YOU'LL BE AT YOUR BEST*⟩⟩

*Way off base = equivocado.

† I'm broke = Estoy en bancarrota.

```
*************************************************
```

[f] as in *FUN, OFFICE,* and *IF*
⟨DICTIONARY MARK: *f*⟩

```
*************************************************
```

PRONOUNCING [f]

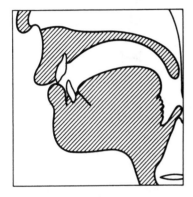

UPPER TEETH:	touch lower lip.
AIRSTREAM:	is continuous without interruption.
VOCAL CORDS:	are not vibrating.

The sound [f] is pronounced the same way as the Spanish letter *f*.

SPANISH KEY WORDS WITH [f]

Spanish words with this sound are spelled with *f*.

> **KEY WORDS:** *feliz*   *enfermo*   *frío*   *café*

POSSIBLE PRONUNCIATION PROBLEMS FOR THE SPANISH SPEAKER

This is a familiar Spanish sound and shouldn't present any difficulty for you in English. Think of the Spanish key word ***café*** and ***your*** [f] ***will be PERFECTLY FINE!***

 **EXERCISE A**

The following words should be pronounced with [f]. Repeat them after your teacher or the instructor on the tape.

[f] **At the Beginning**	[f] **In the Middle**	[f] **At the End**
for	sofa	if
far	offer	off
few	after	life
fast	awful	leaf
from	office	half
free	afraid	safe
five	before	laugh
face	coffee	cough
funny	telephone	photograph

[f] **Spelled:**

"f"	*"ph"*	*"gh"*
fat	phone	rough
fine	phrase	tough
foot	Philip	laugh
first	nephew	cough
stiff	physical	enough
effect	phonetics	
careful	telegraph	

> **HINTS:** 1. The letter *f* is usually pronounced [f].
>
> 2. The letters *ph* are usually pronounced [f].
>
> EXAMPLES: photo telephone graph

EXERCISE B

The boldface words in the following phrases and sentences should be pronounced with [f]. Read them aloud as accurately as possible. **This exercise is not on the tape**.

1. **half** past **four**
2. **before** or **after**
3. **face** the **facts**.
4. I'm **feeling fine**.
5. Do me a **favor**.
6. Answer the **phone**.

7. Are you **free** on **Friday afternoon**?
8. The **office** is on the **first floor**.
9. That **fellow** has a **familiar face**.
10. Do you **prefer fish** or **fowl**?

SELF-TEST I   (Correct answers may be found in the Appendix on p. 207.)

Read the following directions and answer them aloud with the appropriate [f] word from the list. **This self-test is not on the tape**.

graph	photograph	phone	phonetics	philosopher
pharmacy	nephew	phonograph	physician	prophet

1. *Find* another name *for* a drugstore. _____
2. *Find* another name *for* a doctor. _____
3. *Find* another name *for* a snapshot. _____
4. *Find* the name *for* a person who studies *philosophy*. _____
5. *Find* the short *form* of the word *telephone*. _____
6. *Find* another name *for* a record player. _____
7. *Find* the name *for* a person who predicts the *future*. _____
8. *Find* the name *for* the study of sounds. _____
9. *Find* the term that *refers* to your sister's son. _____
10. *Find* the name for a chart showing *figures*. _____

SELF-TEST II (Correct answers may be found in the Appendix on p. 207.)

Read the following paragraph aloud. Circle all words that should be pronounced with the consonant [f]. (Be sure your upper teeth touch your lower
lip as you say [f].) **This self-test is not on the tape**.

. . . .

(Florida) was (founded) by Ponce de Leon in 1513. This famous explorer
from Spain was searching for a fountain of youth. He named the land *Florida*,
which means "full of flowers" in Spanish. He failed in his efforts to find the
fountain. He finally died after fighting the Indians. Unfortunately, no one has
ever found the fountain in Florida or the formula for eternal youth. However,
the fun and sun in Florida are enough to attract folks from every hemisphere
to this famous American state.

. . . .

After checking your answers in the Appendix, read the paragraph aloud one
more time.

FOR AN ENCORE . . .

Reading

Find your horoscope in the local newspaper. Circle all words pronounced with
[f]. Read your *"fortune"* aloud to a friend!

KEEP PRACTICING AND

⟨⟨*YOUR* [f] *WILL BE PERFECTLY FINE*⟩⟩

****

[v] as in *VERY, OVER,* and *SAVE*
⟨DICTIONARY MARK: *v*⟩

****

PRONOUNCING [v]

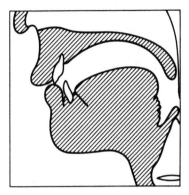

UPPER TEETH: touch the lower lip (as for [f]).

AIRSTREAM: is continuous without interruption.

VOCAL CORDS: are vibrating.

The consonant sound [v] does not exist in most dialects of Spanish.

POSSIBLE PRONUNCIATION PROBLEMS FOR THE SPANISH SPEAKER

1. The Spanish letter *v* is pronounced exactly like *b* (*tuvo* and *tubo* are pronounced the same). As a result, you probably substitute [b] for [v] when speaking English. This will greatly confuse your listeners!

   EXAMPLES: If you say [b] instead of [v]: ***very*** will sound like ***berry***
   vest will sound like ***best***

2. When [v] is the last sound in a word, many Spanish speakers forget to vibrate their vocal cords. This will make [v] sound like [f] and confuse your listeners.

   EXAMPLES: If you say [f] instead of [v]: ***save*** will sound like ***safe***
   leave will sound like ***leaf***

The sound [v] will be easy for you to say if you CONCENTRATE on placing your upper teeth over your bottom lip. ***LOOK IN THE MIRROR* as you practice the [v] exercises** and remember to make your vocal cords vibrate. ***Your* [v] *will be VERY good*!**

 **EXERCISE A**

The following words should be pronounced with [v]. Repeat them after your teacher or the instructor on the tape. (Be sure you feel your upper teeth touch your lower lip.)

[v] **At the Beginning**	[v] **In the Middle**	[v] **At the End**
vine	even	of
vase	over	love
vote	every	live
vest	seven	have
very	cover	move
voice	river	drive
visit	heavy	stove
valley	movie	leave
vowel	clever	carve
vacuum	eleven	brave

> **HINT:** The letter *v* in English is always pronounced [v]. A less common spelling for [v] is the letter *f*.
>
> EXAMPLE: *of*

 EXERCISE B

Repeat the following pairs of words after your teacher or the instructor on the tape. Place your upper teeth over your bottom lip and add voicing for [v]. (Be sure to prolong any vowel BEFORE the sound [v].)

	I		**II**	
[v]	[b]	[v]	[f]
vest	best	save	safe
vow	bow	leave	leaf
very	berry	have	half
marvel	marble	believe	belief
vase	base	calve*	calf†

*Calve = parir la vaca.

† Calf = ternero.

94 [v] as in VERY

EXERCISE C

The boldface words in the following phrases and sentences should be pronounced with the consonant [v]. Repeat them carefully after your teacher or the instructor on the tape.

1. **very** good
2. **very** nice
3. **Very** truly yours
4. Move **over**!
5. **over** and **over**
6. **rivers** and **valleys**

7. Please **vacuum** the **living** room.
8. **Have** you **ever** been to **Venice**?
9. The **vase** is **very heavy**.
10. Did **everyone leave** at **seven**?
11. **Eve** has a **severe fever**.
12. **Move** the **TV over** here.
13. **Vera never** eats **liver**.
14. **Steve** was **five** in **November**.
15. The **movie** got **rave* reviews**!

SELF-TEST I   (Correct answers may be found in the Appendix on p. 207.)

Listen carefully to your teacher or to the tape as 10 words pronounced with [v] are presented. Indicate whether you hear the [v] sound at the **Beginning (B)**, **Middle (M)**, or **END (E)** of the word.

EXAMPLES: A. The instructor says: ***saving***

You circle: B   (M)   E

B. The instructor says: ***value***

You circle: (B)   M   E

1. B   M   E
2. B   M   E
3. B   M   E
4. B   M   E
5. B   M   E

6. B   M   E
7. B   M   E
8. B   M   E
9. B   M   E
10. B   M   E

Rave = hablar con excesivo entusiasmo.

Read the following sentences aloud. Circle the word that correctly completes the sentence. Be sure your vocal cords are vibrating and you feel your top teeth touch your bottom lip as you produce [v]. **This self-test is not on the tape**.

1. (clever   clover   cover)   **Van** is a _____ student.
2. (clever   clover   cover)   I bought a **velvet** _____.
3. (berry   very   ferry)   **Vera** is _____ pretty.
4. (leaf   leave   live)   The train will _____ at **seven**.
5. (leaves   loves   lives)   **Vicky** _____ her sons, **Victor** and **Vance**.

SELF-TEST III   (Correct answers may be found in the Appendix on p. 208.)

Listen carefully to your teacher or to the tape as five three-word series are presented. Only **ONE** word in each series will have the consonant [v]. Circle the number of the word with [v].

EXAMPLE: Your teacher says: *face   vase   base*

You circle: 1   ②   3

1. 1   2   3
2. 1   2   3
3. 1   2   3
4. 1   2   3
5. 1   2   3

SELF-TEST IV
(Correct answers may be found in the Appendix on p. 208.)

Read aloud the following poem by Emily Dickenson. Circle all words that should be pronounced with the consonant [v]. **This self-test is not on the tape**.

I (Never) Saw a Moor

I never saw a moor,
I never saw the sea;
Yet know I how the heather looks,
And what a wave must be.

I never spoke with God,
Nor visited in Heaven;
Yet certain am I of the spot
As if the chart were given.

(Emily Dickenson)

FOR AN ENCORE . . .

Conversation

Everyone likes to be complimented or praised! Plan on complimenting at least five people this week by using such phrases as "*very good*," "*very nice*," "*You look **very** well*," "*You **have** a **very** pretty **vest***," and so on.

KEEP PRACTICING EVERY DAY AND . . . . . .

⟨⟨*YOUR* [v] *WILL BE VERY GOOD!*⟩⟩

****

REVIEW

[p]   [b]   [f]   [v]

****

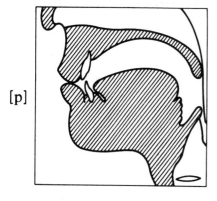

[p]

ENGLISH KEY WORDS: *pay   apple   stop*

The lips are pressed together. The airstream is completely stopped and then released abruptly. The vocal cords are NOT vibrating.

SPANISH KEY WORDS: *poco   papel   esperar*

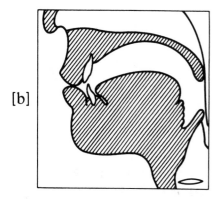

[b]

ENGLISH KEY WORDS: *boy   rabbit   tub*

The lips are pressed together. The airstream is completely stopped and then released abruptly. The vocal cords ARE vibrating.

SPANISH KEY WORDS: *tambien   tambor   combate*

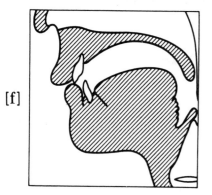

[f]

ENGLISH KEY WORDS: *fall   office   if*

The upper teeth touch the lower lip. The airstream is continuous but the vocal cords are NOT vibrating.

SPANISH KEY WORDS: *feliz   enfermo   frío*

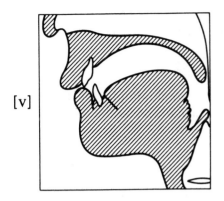

[v]

ENGLISH KEY WORDS: *very   over   save*

The lips are in the same position as for [f]. *The airstream is*
continuous   AND   the   vocal   cords
ARE vibrating.

SPANISH KEY WORDS: — — —

REVIEW EXERCISE

Repeat the rows of words and sentences after your teacher or the instructor
on the tape. Be sure your **lips are together for** [p] **and** [b] and that your
upper teeth touch your lower lip for [f] **and** [v].

[p]	[b]	[f]	[v]
1. **p**at	**b**at	**f**at	**v**at
2. **p**ail	**b**ail	**f**ail	**v**eil
3. **p**an	**b**an	**f**an	**v**an
4. **P**erry	**b**erry	**f**erry	**v**ery
5. **p**ays	**b**ays	**ph**ase	**v**ase

6. The **pail** is big.   The **bale** is big.   The **veil** is big.
7. Who took the **pet**?   Who took the **bet**?   Who took the **vet**?
8. I like the **bays**.   I like the **phase**.   I like the **vase**.
9. It's a small **cup**.   It's a small **cub**.   It's a small **cuff**.
10. Remove the **pan**.   Remove the **ban**.   Remove the **van**.

11. Don't **fail** to **pay** the **bail**.
          [f]   [p]   [b]
12. I **bet** the **vet** will help your **pet**.
       [b]   [v]   [p]
13. **Perry** likes **berry pie very** much.
       [p]   [b]   [p] [v]
14. Get the **pan** and **fan from** the **van**.
              [p]   [f] [f]   [v]
15. Do you **feel** like eating **veal**?
            [f]   [v]

REVIEW TEST I (Correct answers may be found in the Appendix on p. 208.)

Your teacher or the instructor on the tape will present the following sentences using ONE of the words in parentheses. Listen carefully and circle the word (and consonant) used.

EXAMPLE: We bought a new (fan   van).
                                    [f]   [v]

1. Vera took a   (bow   vow).
                          [b]   [v]

2. That's a nice   (beach   peach).
                          [b]   [p]

3. There were a lot of   (boats   votes).
                          [b]   [v]

4. We could see her   (grief   grieve).
                            [f]   [v]

5. I want the   (vest   best).
                          [v]   [b]

6. He got a good   (buy   pie).
                          [b]   [p]

7. Don't cut the   (vine   fine).
                          [v]   [f]

8. The baby sat in his   (lap   lab).
                           [p]   [b]

9. Can you see the   (curb   curve)?
                           [b]   [v]

10. The player picked a (five   fife).
                          [v]   [f]

After checking your answers in the Appendix, read each of the sentences twice. Use the first word in the first reading and the contrast word in the second reading.

 **REVIEW TEST II** <small>(Correct answers may be found in the Appendix on p. 209.)</small>

Listen carefully to your teacher or to the tape as 10 sentences are presented. One word in each sentence will be **INCORRECTLY** pronounced. On the line to the right of each number, write the **CORRECT** word for each sentence.

Sentence   **Correct Word**

EXAMPLE A: ___cub___   (The bear ***cup*** is black and white.)

EXAMPLE B: ___save___   (It's wise to ***safe*** money in a bank.)

1. _____
2. _____
3. _____
4. _____
5. _____
6. _____
7. _____
8. _____
9. _____
10. _____

REVIEW TEST III

(Correct answers may be found in the Appendix on p. 209.)

Read the following definition and **FABLE** aloud. Find all the words pronounced with [p], [b], [f], or [v] and write them under the appropriate phonetic symbols. **This review test is not on the tape**.

Definition of _fable_: A fable is a story that teaches a valuable lesson. Aesop's fables are very well known. His brief stories tell of the faults and virtues of people.

. . . .

The Fox and the Grapes

Once there was a very hungry fox. He saw some fine grapes hanging above from a vine. He tried jumping up, but he couldn't reach the grapes. Finally, he became furious and gave up. As he left, the fox said, "I didn't really want those grapes. They were probably sour!"

(by Aesop)

. . . .

The next time somebody pretends he doesn't want something because he really can't have it, you can say "sour grapes!"

[p]	[b]	[f]	[v]
	fable	definition fable	of

```
************************************************
```

[k] as in *CAKE*, *CAR*, and *BOOK*

⟨DICTIONARY MARK: *k*⟩

```
************************************************
```

PRONOUNCING [k]

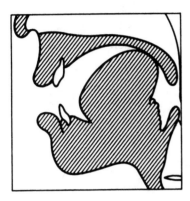

BACK OF TONGUE: touches the soft palate.

AIRSTREAM: is stopped and then exploded.

VOCAL CORDS: are not vibrating.

The sound [k] in English is similar to the sound of the letters *c* or *k* in certain Spanish words. (The English [k] is aspirate and is produced with a strong puff of air.)

SPANISH KEY WORDS WITH [k]

Spanish words with this sound are spelled with *c* or *k*.

> **KEY WORDS:** *como*   *casa*   *acá*   *kilo*

POSSIBLE PRONUNCIATION PROBLEMS FOR THE SPANISH SPEAKER

This is an easy consonant for you to say. Just remember that [k] is more explosive in English than in Spanish. When it begins a word, it must be said with strong aspiration and a puff of air.* ***KEEP PRACTICING. You CAN say*** [k̲] ***OK̲***!

*When *k* follows *s* (as in *sky*, *skin*, *skate*, etc.), it is **NOT** aspirated with a puff of air.

 **EXERCISE A**

The following words should be pronounced with [k]. Repeat them after your teacher or the instructor on the tape.

[k] **At the Beginning**	[k] **In the Middle**	[k] **At the End**
can	cookie	like
car	become	took
key	record	week
cold	jacket	sick
keep	inquire	work
come	walking	make
quick	because	clock
could	mechanic	speak
correct	backward	black

[k] **Spelled:**

"*k*"	"*c*"	"*qu*" ([kw])	"*x*" ([ks])
kite	coat	quit	six
kill	cone	quick	box
lake	acre	quiet	wax
keep	class	quote	exit
bake	crime	square	mixture

A less frequent spelling pattern for [k] consists of the letters *ch*.

EXAMPLES: chorus   chrome   mechanic   Christmas

> ***HINTS:***   1. The most common spelling pattern for [k] is *k*.
>
>   2. The letters *qu* are usually pronounced [kw].
>   EXAMPLES: queen   quite   require
>
>   3. The letter *c* before *a, o,* or *u* is usually pronounced [k].
>   EXAMPLES: cap   because   comb   become   cut
>
>   4. The letter *k* followed by *n* is usually **NOT** pronounced.
>   EXAMPLES: knit [nɪt]   knot [nɑt]   know [noʊ]

EXERCISE B

Read the following phrases and sentences aloud. Be sure to pronounce any [k] at the beginning of the boldface words with a puff of air. **This exercise is not on the tape**.

1. **Keep quiet**!
2. **milk** and **cookies**
3. **call** it **quits**

4. **cup** of **coffee**
5. **Can** I **come** in?
6. **Speak clearly**.

7. I **like black coffee**.
8. **Carol** is **working** as a **cook**.
9. **Pack** your **clothes** for the **weekend**.
10. **Keep accurate records**.

SELF-TEST I   (Correct answers may be found in the Appendix on p. 210.)

Read each four-word series aloud. Circle the **ONE** word in each group of four that is NOT pronounced with [k]. **This self-test is not on the tape**.

EXAMPLE:	rice	rack	rake	wreck
1.	course	count	choose	chorus
2.	can't	can	cent	cone
3.	Canada	Texas	Kansas	Massachusetts
4.	key	keep	keen	kneel
5.	celery	corn	carrots	cabbage
6.	mix	box	explain	xylophone
7.	knee	back	ankle	cheek
8.	Charles	Carol	Chris	Michael
9.	mechanic	much	chrome	Christmas
10.	milk	cider	coffee	cream

SELF-TEST II (Correct answers may be found in the Appendix on p. 210.)

Read the following paragraph aloud. Circle all words that should be pronounced with [k]. **This self-test is not on the tape.**

....

The American Cowboy

Americans created the name *cowboy* for the men who cared for the cattle. You might recall the typical singing cowboy in the movies. He was kind, courageous, and good-looking. He always caught the cow, colt, and of course, the girl! But the real cowboy was a hard worker who had many difficult tasks. He had to take the cattle to market. These lonely cattle drives took many weeks through rough country. The cowboy had to protect the cattle and keep them from running off. In fact or fiction, the cowboy will continue to be a likeable American character. **Ride 'em cowboy!**

....

After checking your answers in the Appendix, practice reading "**The American Cowboy**" again.

FOR AN ENCORE . . .

Conversation

Ask new people you meet, "What **kind** of **work** do you do?" Every time you ask for a "**cup** of **black coffee**" or "**coffee** with **milk** or **cream**," **carefully** pronounce [k]!

KEEP PRACTICING AND . . . . . .

⟨⟨*YOU CAN SAY* [k] *OK*⟩⟩

```
*********************************************
```

[g] as in *GO*, *BEGIN*, and *EGG*
⟨DICTIONARY MARK: *g*⟩

```
*********************************************
```

PRONOUNCING [g]

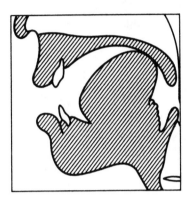

BACK OF TONGUE: touches the soft palate.

AIRSTREAM: is stopped and then exploded.

VOCAL CORDS: are vibrating.

The sound [g] in English is similar to the sound of the Spanish letter *g* after *n* or before *a*, *o*, *u*, or *r* in certain Spanish words. (English [g] is more explosive than Spanish *g*.)

SPANISH KEY WORDS WITH [g]

Spanish words with this sound are spelled with *g*.

KEY WORDS: *tengo   gato   guerra   grande*

POSSIBLE PRONUNCIATION PROBLEMS
FOR THE SPANISH SPEAKER

This is another easy consonant for you to say. However, when [g] is the last sound in a word, you might forget to add voicing. This will make [g] sound like [k] and change the meaning of your word.

EXAMPLES: If you substitute [k] for [g]:   **bag** will sound like **back**
dug will sound like **duck**

Always make your vocal cords vibrate for [g], especially at the end of words. Let your [g] **GO** with an explosion. ***Your* [g] *has* GOT *to be* GOOD**!

 **EXERCISE A**

The following words should be pronounced with [g]. Repeat them after your teacher or the instructor on the tape. Be sure to make your vocal cords vibrate.

[g] **At the Beginning**	[g] **In the Middle**	[g] **At the End**
go	cigar	beg
get	agree	pig
girl	begin	bag
gone	anger	rug
great	forget	log
guess	bigger	dog
green	hungry	egg
glass	beggar	drug
gather	cigarette	flag

[g] **Spelled:**

"g"	**"x"** ([gz])
go	exact
give	exam
game	example
forgive	exert
regain	exhibit

EXERCISE B

Read aloud the following pairs of words. (Be sure to make your vocal cords vibrate for [g] and to prolong any vowel BEFORE the sound [g].) **This exercise is not on the tape**.

[g]	[k]
bag	back
pig	pick
log	lock
dug	duck
tag	tack

EXERCISE C

The boldface words in the following phrases and sentences should be pronounced with [g]. Read them aloud as accurately as possible. **This exercise is not on the tape**.

1. **good** night
2. I don't **agree**.
3. Where are you **going**?
4. **begin again**
5. a **good girl**
6. a **big dog**

7. **Peggy** is **going** to the **game**.
8. The **dog dug** up his bone **again**.
9. Don't kill the **goose** that lays the **golden egg**.
10. There's a **big bug** on the **rug**.

 **SELF-TEST I**   (Correct answers may be found in the Appendix on p. 210.)

Your teacher or the instructor on the tape will say only ONE word in each of the following pairs. Listen carefully and circle the word you hear.

EXAMPLES: A. (wig)   wick

          B. tug   (tuck)

1. lag   lack
2. bug   buck
3. league   leak
4. peg   peck
5. nag   knack

SELF-TEST II (Correct answers may be found in the Appendix on p. 211.)

Mr. and Mrs. **Green** are planning a menu for their **guests**. Only foods pronounced with [g] will be served. Read the menu aloud and circle all items pronounced with [g]. **This self-test is not on the tape.**

BREAKFAST

Grapefruit   Fried Eggs   Grits   Sausage

LUNCH

Hamburgers   Grilled Onions   Gelatin   Vinegar Dressing

COCKTAILS

Margarita   Gin and Tonic   Sangria   Grand Marnier

DINNER

Lasagna   Leg of Lamb   Green Peas   Chicken Gumbo Soup

DESSERT

Angel Food Cake   Glazed Doughnuts   Grapes   Figs

After checking your answers in the Appendix, practice each circled [g] menu item by saying it in the sentence *"I'm __GOING__ to eat* _____*."* **Be sure to pronounce all [g] menu items correctly!**

FOR AN ENCORE . . .

Conversation

Every time you use the word **GOOD** in conversation (**"Good** morning," "You look **good**," "Did you have a **good** time?" etc.) be sure to pronounce [g] correctly.

《YOUR [g] has GOT TO BE GOOD》

****

[w] as in *WE* and *AWAY*
⟨DICTIONARY MARK: *w*⟩

****

PRONOUNCING [w]

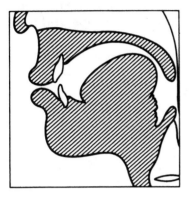

LIPS: are rounded and in the same position as for the vowel [u].

AIRSTREAM: is continuous.

VOCAL CORDS: are vibrating.

The sound [w] is similar to the sound of the Spanish letters *u* after *c*, *g*, or *b* (as in *cuando, antiguo, abuela*) or *hu* (*huele, hueso*) in many dialects of Spanish.

SPANISH KEY WORDS WITH [w]

Spanish words with this sound are spelled with *u* or *hu*.

    KEY WORDS: *cuando*   *antiguo*   *hueso*   *huele*

POSSIBLE PRONUNCIATION PROBLEMS FOR THE SPANISH SPEAKER

The sound [w] frequently alternates with [g] in many dialects of Spanish. For example, some speakers often say either [gueso] **or** [weso] for *hueso*. If you pronounce English [w] with the harsh forceful quality that some Spanish speakers use for *hu*, it will sound like you are saying a [g] before the [w].

EXAMPLES: If you say [g] before [w]:   ***want*** will sound like "***gwant***"
                                               when will sound like "***gwen***"

Remember to round your lips as you say [w]. You should feel all speech movements in the **FRONT** of your mouth, *not* the back. ***Don't WORRY! Keep WORKING AWAY and your* [w] *WILL be WONDERFUL!***

EXERCISE A

The following words should be pronounced with [w]. Repeat them after your teacher or the instructor on the tape. ***Be sure to round your lips and feel ALL movement in the <u>front</u> of your mouth!***
(The consonant [w] does not occur at the end of words in English.)

[w] **In the Beginning**	[w] **In the Middle**
we	away
was	awake
want	always
word	anyway
work	beware
wait	between
wool	someone
would	quick
women	choir
winter	

Less frequent spelling patterns for [w] consist of the letters *o* and *u*.

EXAMPLES: <u>o</u>ne any<u>o</u>ne q<u>u</u>een q<u>u</u>iet

HINTS: 1. The letter *w* is always pronounced [w] when followed by a vowel in the same syllable.

   EXAMPLES: <u>w</u>ood <u>w</u>ill back<u>w</u>ard high<u>w</u>ay

  2. The letter *w* at the end of a word is always *silent*.

   EXAMPLES: how sew law know

NOTE: Some English speakers use [hw] when pronouncing words spelled with *wh*: *when, where, white, wheel, awhile, somewhat*. They use aspiration and sound as if they are saying [h] before the [w]. In this manual, the use of either [w] or [hw] will be acceptable when pronouncing words spelled with *wh*.

EXERCISE B

The boldface words in the following phrases and sentences should be pronounced with [w]. Read them aloud as accurately as possible. **This exercise is not on the tape**.

1. **What** do you **want**?
2. You're **welcome**.
3. **Where will** you be?
4. **Walk quickly**.
5. **Where** is it?
6. **Waste** not, **want** not!

7. **Which one** do you **want**?
8. **What was** the **question**?
9. The **women were wearing white**.
10. **Walt always works** on **Wednesday**.

SELF-TEST I   (Correct answers may be found in the Appendix on p. 211.)

Read each of the following words aloud. Circle only the words that are pronounced with [w]. **This self-test is not on the tape**.

week	someone	queen	write
while	who	wrong	worry
whose	waiter	reward	square
guilt	unwilling	saw	worthy
west	lawyer	anywhere	low

SELF-TEST II

(Correct answers may be found in the Appendix on p. 211.)

Read the following paragraph about **Woodrow Wilson** aloud. Circle all words that should be pronounced with [w]. **This self-test is not on the tape**.

$\widehat{\text{Woodrow}}$ $\widehat{\text{Wilson}}$

Woodrow Wilson was the twenty-fifth president of the United States. He will always be remembered for his work to establish world peace. Wilson was born in 1865 and later went to Princeton University. He became president in 1913 and stayed in the White House for two terms. His first wife died while he was in office, and he married a Washington widow. When the United States entered World War I in 1917, Wilson quickly provided the needed wisdom. After the war, Wilson made a nationwide tour to win support for the League of Nations. Wilson was awarded the Nobel Prize for his worthwhile work for peace. He died in 1924. Everywhere in the world, Wilson was thought of as a wise and wonderful leader.

SELF-TEST III

(Correct answers may be found in the Appendix on p. 212.)

Read the following questions about **Woodrow Wilson** aloud. Fill in the blanks with the correct answers. **Be sure to pronounce all [w] words correctly**. **This self-test is not on the tape**.

1. **When was Woodrow Wilson** born?
   Woodrow Wilson was born in _____.
2. How many **wives** did **Wilson** have **while** in the **White** House?
   Wilson had _____ **wives**.
3. **When** did the United States enter **World War I**?
   The United States entered **World War I** in _____.
4. **Why was Wilson awarded** the Nobel Prize?
   Wilson was awarded the Nobel Prize for his _____.
5. **Where was Wilson** thought of as a **wise and wonderful** leader?
   Wilson was thought of as a **wise and wonderful** leader _____.

FOR AN ENCORE . . .

Conversation

Most questions begin with the [w] sound. **ALWAYS** pronounce [w] correctly when you ask **Where? When? Why? Which** one? **Will** you? **Won't** you? and so on.

KEEP WORKING AND

《 *YOUR* [w] *WILL BE WONDERFUL* 》

```
****************************************************
```

[l] as in *LAMP, YELLOW*, and *POOL*

⟨DICTIONARY MARK: *l*⟩

```
****************************************************
```

PRONOUNCING [l]

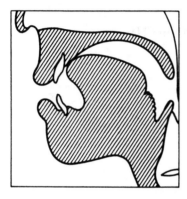

TONGUE TIP:	**is pressed against gum ridge behind upper front teeth.**
AIRSTREAM:	**is continuous and passes over both sides of the tongue.**
VOCAL CORDS:	**are vibrating.**

The sound [l] in English is similar to the sound of the Spanish letter "*l*".

SPANISH KEY WORDS WITH [l]

Spanish words with this sound are spelled with "*l*".

    KEY WORDS: *linda*   *lana*   *calma*   *falso*   *malo*

POSSIBLE PRONUNCIATION PROBLEMS
FOR THE SPANISH SPEAKER

This is a familiar Spanish sound and shouldn't present any difficulty for you in English. *LEARN your LESSONS WELL; You WILL say a perfect* [l]!

EXERCISE A

The following words should be pronounced with [l]. Repeat them after your teacher or the instructor on the tape. Remember "*ll*" in English is pronounced like *l* in *Linda*.

[l] **At the Beginning**　　[l] **In the Middle**

[l] At the Beginning	[l] In the Middle
let	only
leg	alone
live	alive
late	hello
last	salad
long	asleep
light	family
leave	yellow
learn	balloon
little	believe

EXERCISE B

When *l* is the last sound in a word, the back of the tongue should be raised higher than for *l* at the beginning or in the middle of words. (In Spanish, "*l*" is pronounced the same regardless of whether it begins or ends a word.) Repeat the following words after your teacher or the instructor on the tape. **Be sure to raise the back of your tongue higher in the mouth toward the soft palate**.

[l] **At the End**

all	able
tell	apple
fill	table
call	people
fool	trouble

NOTE ABOUT "SYLLABIC [l]":   When an unstressed syllable begins with [t] or [d] and ends with [l], the [l] is frequently pronounced as "syllabic [l]." It is formed by keeping the tongue tip on the upper gum ridge without moving it from the position of the preceding [t] or [d].

EXAMPLES: paddle   little   bottle   saddle   idle   noodle

EXERCISE C

The boldface words in the following phrases and sentences should be pronounced with [l]. Read them aloud as accurately as possible. **This exercise is not on the tape**.

1. **telephone call**
2. **Leave** me **alone**.
3. **lots** of **luck**
4. **Light** the **candle**.
5. **Please believe** me.
6. **Learn** your **lesson**.

7. **Will** you **mail** the **letter**?
8. The **little girl fell asleep**.
9. **Lucy lost** her **locket**.
10. He who **laughs last, laughs** best!

SELF-TEST I   (Correct answers may be found in the Appendix on p. 212.)

Read the following sentences aloud. Fill in the blanks with the correct [l] country or state. **This self-test is not on the tape**.

EXAMPLE: If you are *located* in *Baltimore*, you *live* in **MARYLAND**.

1. If you are *located* in *Dublin*, you *live* in _____.
2. If you are *located* in *London*, you *live* in _____.
3. If you are *located* in *Los Angeles*, you *live* in _____.
4. If you are *located* in *Lisbon*, you *live* in _____.
5. If you are *located* in *Lucerne*, you *live* in _____.
6. If you are *located* in *Milan*, you *live* in _____.
7. If you are *located* in *São Paolo*, you *live* in _____.
8. If you are *located* in *Brussels*, you *live* in _____.
9. If you are *located* in *Orlando*, you *live* in _____.
10. If you are *located* in *New Orleans*, you *live* in _____.

SELF-TEST II (Correct answers may be found in the Appendix on p. 212.)

Read the following dialogue aloud. Circle all words pronounced with [l]. **This self-test is not on the tape**.

. . . .

LILLIAN: (Allan,) I just had a (telephone) call from Aunt Lola. Uncle Bill died.

ALLAN: The uncle who was a millionaire?

LILLIAN: Yes. He lived alone in California.

ALLAN: Did he leave us any money?

LILLIAN: The lawyer is reading the will at 11:00. I really don't believe he left his family anything!

ALLAN: Uncle Bill had to leave something to a relative.

LILLIAN: He lived with lots of animals. He didn't like people.

ALLAN: Hold it! I'll answer the telephone. (*Allan hangs up the phone.*) Well, Lillian, you're out of luck! Uncle Bill left all his "loot"* to the Animal Lovers' League.

LILLIAN: Do you think Lulu, our poodle, is eligible for a little?

. . . .

FOR AN ENCORE . . .

Reading

Look in the classified section of the newspaper. Circle all words pronounced with [l] in at least three want ads. Read them aloud.

Conversation

Everyone **likes** a **compliment**! **Compliment** at **least** five **people** you know with "I like your new blouse" or "Blue looks lovely on you!", etc.

⟨⟨LEARN TO SAY [l] WELL!⟩⟩

*Loot = dinero.

```
*****************************************************
```

[r] as in *RED, MARRY,* and *FAR*
⟨DICTIONARY MARK: *r*⟩

```
*****************************************************
```

PRONOUNCING [r]

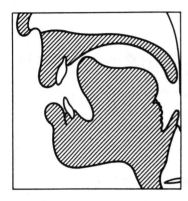

TONGUE TIP: is curled upward but does NOT touch the roof of the mouth.

AIRSTREAM: is continuous.

VOCAL CORDS: are vibrating.

POSSIBLE PRONUNCIATION PROBLEMS FOR THE SPANISH SPEAKER

The sound [r] as it is pronounced in English does not exist in Spanish. The Spanish *r* is trilled and is produced by rapidly touching your tongue tip to the upper gum ridge one or more times. You probably use the Spanish *r* when speaking English. This will not change the meaning of words but will contribute to a "foreign-sounding" accent.

Make sure that your tongue tip **NEVER** touches your upper gum ridge and you will pronounce English [r] correctly. *REMEMBER to PRACTICE* [r] *CAREFULLY; YOUR* [r] *will be RIGHT on TARGET!*

EXERCISE A

The following words should be pronounced with [r]. Repeat them carefully after your teacher or the instructor on the tape. **Be sure your tongue does NOT touch your upper gum ridge when you say** [r].

[r] At the Beginning	[r] In the Middle	[r] At the End
red	very	or
run	marry	are
row	story	far
read	berry	door
rest	sorry	near
rich	hurry	more
rain	carrot	sure
real	orange	their
wrong	around	before
write	tomorrow	appear

EXERCISE B

The boldface words in the following phrases and sentences should be pronounced with [r]. Repeat them carefully after your teacher or the instructor on the tape.

1. **Where are** you?
2. **near or far**
3. **Are** you **sure**?
4. See you **tomorrow**.
5. I'm **very sorry**.
6. He'll be **right there**.

7. **Roy returns tomorrow morning**.
8. The **train arrives every hour**.
9. I **already read** that **short story**.
10. **Rose** is **wearing** a **red dress**.
11. **Robert ran around** the **corner**.
12. **Rita** and **Larry are married**.
13. **Remember, never** put the **cart before** the **horse**!*
14. **Mark** couldn't **start** the **car**.
15. I **rented** a **four-room apartment**.

To put the cart before the horse = empezar la casa por el tejado.

SELF-TEST I   (Correct answers may be found in the Appendix on p. 213.)

Read the following sentences aloud. Fill in the blanks with the name of the correct [r] "creature." **This self-test is not on the tape**.

1. This **creature** has black and white **stripes**. This **creature** is a _____

2. This **forest creature** has long **ears** and is a **celebrity** at **Easter**. This **creature** is a _____.

3. This **creature** has **large antlers** and is **around** at **Christmas**. This **creature** is a _____.

4. This **creature** has spots and a **very** long neck. This **creature** is a _____.

5. This **creature** lives in the **arctic**, is **large**, and is **very hungry**. This **creature** is a **polar** _____.

6. This **forest creature carries her** babies in a pouch. This **creature** is a _____.

7. This **friendly creature "croaks"** and says **"rivet, rivet**." This **creature** is a _____.

8. This **forest creature** is a **very** talkative **bird**. This **colorful creature** is a _____.

9. This **fierce creature** has black and yellow **stripes**. This **ferocious creature** is a _____.

10. This **graceful creature started** as a **caterpillar**. This **pretty creature** is a _____.

SELF-TEST II

(Correct answers may be found in the Appendix on p. 213.)

Read the following paragraph about **Robin Hood** aloud. Circle all words pronounced with [r]. (*Remember, don't let your tongue tip touch the upper gum ridge.*) **This self-test is not on the tape**.

....

(Robin) Hood

The story of Robin Hood has been retold many times. Robin Hood was an outlaw who lived in Sherwood Forest. He lived there with Maid Marian, Friar Tuck, and others. Robin was really a hero rather than a criminal. He robbed the rich and gave to the poor. He was a remarkable marksman with his bow and arrow. The story of Robin Hood has been written about and dramatized since the eleventh century. Robin truly represents a righteous figure opposing cruelty and greed.

....

After checking your answers in the Appendix, practice reading about **Robin Hood** again.

FOR AN ENCORE . . .

Conversation

Get off to the **right start** with [r]! Try to use the word **RIGHT** in as many expressions as possible, for example, "I'll be **right** with you," "All **right**," "*Do you have the **right** time?*" "*That's **right**!*" and so on. **Be sure to pronounce [r] correctly!**

REMEMBER TO PRACTICE [r] CAREFULLY AND . . . . . .

⟪ *YOUR* [r] *WILL BE RIGHT!* ⟫

****

[h] as in *HAT* and *BEHIND*
⟨DICTIONARY MARK: *h*⟩

****

PRONOUNCING [h]

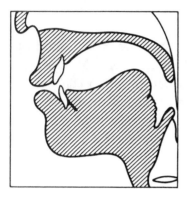

TONGUE: glides into position for whichever vowel follows [h].

AIRSTREAM: is continuous.

VOCAL CORDS: are not vibrating.

The sound [h] is similar to the sound of the Spanish letters *g* before *e* or *i* (as in *gente* or *girar*) and *j* (*jota*) in several dialects of American Spanish. The use of [h] is most evident in the Spanish of Central America, the Caribbean, Colombia, and Venezuela.

SPANISH KEY WORDS WITH [h]

Spanish words with this sound are spelled with *j*, *g*, and sometimes *x*.

    KEY WORDS: *jugar*   *mujer*   *gente*   *Mexico*

POSSIBLE PRONUNCIATION PROBLEMS FOR THE SPANISH SPEAKER

1. The Spanish letter *h* is silent. As a result, Spanish speakers may omit it in English.

    EXAMPLES: If you leave out [h]:   ***hat***   will sound like ***at***
                                                hand will sound like ***and***

2. Since [h] might not exist in your dialect of Spanish, you might pronounce it with the harsh forceful quality that some Spanish speakers normally use when saying *g* or *j*.

This is a very easy sound to produce. Relax your throat and tongue; GENTLY let out a puff of air as if you were sighing! **Work <u>H</u>ARD and you'll be <u>H</u>APPY with** [h]!

 **EXERCISE A**

The following words should be pronounced with [h]. Repeat them after your teacher or the instructor on the tape. *(Remember—let out a GENTLE puff of air as you say* [h].)

[h] **At the Beginning**	[h] **In the Middle**
he	ahead
how	behind
who	behave
here	inhale
heat	anyhow
have	unhappy
home	perhaps
hello	inherit
heart	rehearse

A less frequent spelling pattern for [h] is *wh*.

EXAMPLES: who   whom   whose   whole

> **HINTS:** 1. The letter *h* is silent when it follows *g*, *k*, or *r* at the beginning of words.
>
>   EXAMPLES: ghost khaki rhubarb
>
> 2. The letter *h* is always silent in the words *honest, heir, honor,* and *hour.*

EXERCISE B

Read aloud the following pairs of words. (Be sure to distinguish between the word pairs by letting out a gentle puff of air when saying [h].) **This exercise is not on the tape**.

I	II
hi	I
hit	it
hat	at
hate	ate
heat	eat

EXERCISE C

Read the following phrases and sentences aloud. The boldface words should be pronounced with [h]. **This exercise is not on the tape**.

1. **Hurry** up!
2. What **happened**?
3. **Who** is it?
4. **hand** in **hand**
5. **How have** you been?
6. You **hit** the nail on the **head**!*

7. **Henry hit** a **home** run.
8. **He had hot** dogs and **hamburgers**.
9. **Who** lives **behind** the **house**?
10. **Helen has** brown **hair**.
11. **Her home** is in **Ohio**.
12. **Have** you **heard** from **Harry**?
13. **He hurt his hand**.
14. I **hate hot** and **humid** weather.
15. **Heaven helps** those **who help** themselves.

Hit the nail on head = dar en el clavo.

SELF-TEST I

(Correct answers may be found in the Appendix on p. 213.)

Guess what? You're **HAVING** a **HOLIDAY**! Plan your tour by circling the places pronounced with [h]. **This self-test is not on the tape**.

(Ohio)   Michigan   Oklahoma   Houston
Idaho   Massachusetts   Washington   New Hampshire
Chicago   Hartford   Hawaii   Tallahassee

After checking your answers in the Appendix, practice the names of these places by using them in the sentence "*I'm **having** a **holiday** in* _____."

SELF-TEST II

(Correct answers may be found in the Appendix on p. 214.)

Read the following dialogue aloud. Circle all words pronounced with [h]. **This self-test is not on the tape**.

. . . .

HELEN: (Hi,) Mom. Welcome (home.) How was Hawaii?
MOTHER: Like a second honeymoon! I'm as happy as a lark.* How are you?
HELEN: Horrible! Henry is in the hospital with a broken hip.
MOTHER: How did that happen?
HELEN: He heard a noise outside. He went behind the house and fell over a hose.
MOTHER: How are my handsome grandsons?
HELEN: They won't behave. And my housekeeper had to quit.
MOTHER: Perhaps you'd like me to help at home.
HELEN: Oh, Mom, I was hoping you'd say that. Hurry to the house as soon as possible.
MOTHER: I guess the honeymoon is over. Here we go again!

. . . .

After checking your answers in the Appendix, read the dialogue again. Be sure to aspirate all [h] words with a gentle puff of air.

Happy as a lark = estar más alegre que una pascua.

FOR AN ENCORE . . .

Conversation

You can get lots of practice using [h] when greeting people. Pronounce [h] carefully when you say **Hi**, **Hello**, **How** are you? **How's** your family? **Hope** to see you soon, and so on

《**DO YOUR HOMEWORK AND YOU'LL BE HAPPY WITH** [h]》

****

REVIEW

[k] [g] [w] [l] [r] [h]

****

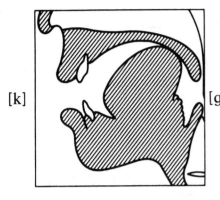

[k] [g]

[k] **ENGLISH KEY WORDS:** *cake car book*
[g] **ENGLISH KEY WORDS:** *go begin egg*

The back of the tongue presses against the soft palate. The airstream is stopped and then exploded. The vocal cords DON'T vibrate for [k]; they DO vibrate for [g].

[k] **SPANISH KEY WORDS:** *como casa kilo*
[g] **SPANISH KEY WORDS:** *tengo gato guerra*

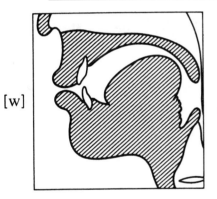

[w]

ENGLISH KEY WORDS: *we away*

The lips are very rounded. All movements are felt in the FRONT of the mouth. The airstream is continuous and the vocal cords ARE vibrating.

SPANISH KEY WORDS: *cuando hueso abuela*

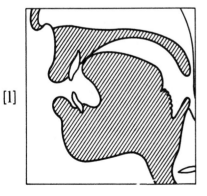

[l]

ENGLISH KEY WORDS: *lamp yellow pool*

The tongue tip is pressed against the upper gum ridge. The airstream is continuous and passes over both sides of the tongue. The vocal cords ARE vibrating.

SPANISH KEY WORDS: *linda calma malo*

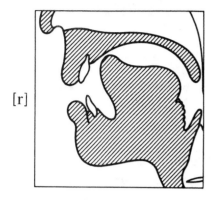

[r]

ENGLISH KEY WORDS: *red   marry   far*

The tongue tip is curled upward but does not touch the roof of the mouth. The airstream is continuous and the vocal cords ARE vibrating.

SPANISH KEY WORDS: — — —

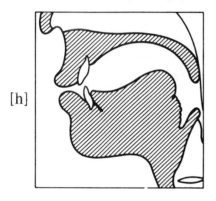

[h]

ENGLISH KEY WORDS: *how   hat   behind*

[h] is an aspirate sound and must be produced with a gentle puff of air. The airstream is continuous and the vocal cords are NOT vibrating.

SPANISH KEY WORDS: *jugar   gente   Mexico*

REVIEW EXERCISE

Repeat the rows of words and sentences after your teacher or the instructor on the tape.

[l]	[r]	[h]
1. lay	ray	hay
2. low	row	hoe
3. light	right	height
4. led	red	head
5. late	rate	hate

[k]	[g]	[w]
6. call	gall	wall
7. kill	gill	will
8. could	good	wood
9. cane	gain	Wayne
10. curl	girl	whirl

11. Did they **leap**?   Did they **reap**?   Did they **weep**?
     [l]   [r]   [w]

12. Take your **pill**.   Take your **pick**.   Take your **pig**.
     [l]   [k]   [g]

13. **Lead** them.   **Read** them.   **Weed** them.   **Heed** them.
   [l]   [r]   [w]   [h]

14. Look at the **light**. Look at the **right**. Look at the **white**.
           [l]   [r]   [w]

15. He **led** yesterday. He **read** yesterday. He **wed** yesterday.
    [l]   [r]   [w]

16. The ***white light*** looks ***right***.
    [w]   [l]   [l]   [r]

17. ***Mac*** put the ***rag*** on the ***rack***.
    [k]   [g]   [k]

18. He ***rode*** with a heavy ***load***.
   [h] [r]   [w]   [h]   [l]

19. Drive safely and ***arrive alive***!
   [r]   [l]   [r]   [l]

20. Don't ***wait*** for the ***crime rate*** to ***climb***.
     [w]   [r]   [r]   [l]

REVIEW TEST I   (Correct answers may be found in the Appendix on p. 214.)

Your teacher or the instructor on the tape will present the following sentences using only ONE of the words in parentheses. Listen carefully and circle the word (and sound) used.

EXAMPLE: Larry likes to ((read)   weed).
                                [r]   [w]

1. Leave it in the (back   bag).
                          [k]   [g]
2. I think it's (good   wood).
                   [g]   [w]
3. Do you like the (rhyme   lime)?
                        [r]   [l]
4. His name is (Gil   Will).
                   [g]   [w]
5. She needs a bigger (lock   log).
                            [k]   [g]
6. Turn toward the (light   right).
                       [l]   [r]
7. They really (ate   hate) the cake.
                        [h]
8. My teacher (collected   corrected) the papers.
                    [l]   [r]
9. Give him the (coat   goat).
                    [k]   [g]
10. Who asked for (jelly   Jerry)?
                      [l]   [r]

After checking your answers in the Appendix, read each of the sentences twice. Carefully pronounce the first word in parentheses in the first reading and the contrast word in the second reading.

REVIEW TEST II

Read the following words aloud. Write each word under the symbol that represents the consonant sound of the boldface letter(s). **This review test is not on the tape**.

grass	s**qu**are	e**x**plain	**wr**itten	**wh**ole	a**w**ake
coast	**wh**ose	o**n**e	**w**e	pour	**qu**eer
blame	there	some**h**ow	ti**ck**et	**ch**orus	**gh**ost
in**h**ale	re**g**ular	sim**pl**e	fi**x**	**w**eather	**l**isten
kitten	mea**l**	**l**eague	bra**g**	bi**ll**ion	**wr**ist
bra**v**e	**wr**ite	history	**w**estern	sa**l**ad	**w**ind

[k] **as in** cake	[g] **as in** go	[l] **as in** lamp	[r] **as in** red	[w] **as in** we	[h] **as in** hat
_____	grass	_____	_____	square	_____
_____	_____	_____	_____	_____	_____
_____	_____	_____	_____	_____	_____
_____	_____	_____	_____	_____	_____
_____	_____	_____	_____	_____	_____
_____	_____	_____	_____	_____	_____
_____	_____	_____	_____	_____	_____

After checking your answers in the Appendix, carefully pronounce the preceding words one more time.

Find **ALL** words pronounced with **one** or **more** of our target sounds. Circle the letter(s) representing those sounds and write the number of the phonetic symbol that corresponds to the sound above the letter(s). Then identify the name of the person described in each paragraph. **This review test is not on the tape**.

Pronunciation Key:

1 = [k] as in *cake*	4 = [l] as in *lamp*
2 = [g] as in *go*	5 = [r] as in *red*
3 = [w] as in *we*	6 = [h] as in *hat*

. . . .

⁶(H)e ³(w)as ³(o)ne of the ³(w)o⁵(r)⁴(l)d's ²(g)⁵(r)eatest a⁵(r)tists. ⁶(H)e ³(w)as bo⁵(r)n in Greece but did most of his work in Spain. His religious paintings are haunting and original. His painting "View of Toledo" is a brilliant landscape. He lived in the sixteenth century. The name of this great artist is _____.

. . . .

She was the famous queen of the Nile. She was loved by Julius Caesar and lived with him in Rome. Later, she married Marc Antony and caused his downfall. She took her own life with the bite of a snake. She is a leading character is many great literary works. The name of this world famous person is _____.

. . . .

```
***********************************************************
```

[m] **as in** *ME* **and** *SWIM*   [n] **as in** *NO* **and** *RUN*
⟨DICTIONARY MARK: *m*⟩   ⟨DICTIONARY MARK: *n*⟩

[ŋ] **as in** *SING*
⟨DICTIONARY MARK: ŋ⟩

```
***********************************************************
```

PRONOUNCING [m]

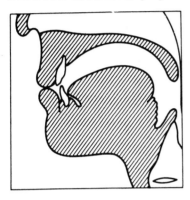

LIPS:	are together in a "humming" position.
AIRSTREAM:	is continuous through the nose.
VOCAL CORDS:	are vibrating.

The sound [m] is pronounced the same as the Spanish letter *m*.

SPANISH KEY WORDS WITH [m]

Spanish words with this sound are spelled with *m*.

   KEY WORDS: *mama*   *comer*   *tambien*

POSSIBLE PRONUNCIATION PROBLEMS
FOR THE SPANISH SPEAKER

This is a familiar sound to you; it will be easy to say in the beginning and middle of words. However, [m] does not occur at the end of words in Spanish. You might substitute the more familiar [n] or [ŋ] at the end of the words in English.

EXAMPLES: If you say [n] instead of [m]:   ***some*** will become ***sun***
            If you say [ŋ] instead of [m]:   ***swim*** will become ***swing***

Remember, make your lips come together in a "humming" position for [m]. *Say "mmmmmmmmmm" and your* [m] *will be marvelous*!

 **EXERCISE A**

The following words should be pronounced with [m]. Repeat them after your teacher or the instructor on the tape. (*Remember—lips together!*)

[m] **At the Beginning**	[m] **In the Middle**	[m] **At the End**
me	army	am
may	among	him
mat	lemon	them
more	animal	seem
milk	camera	name
mean	summer	time
month	hammer	room
matter	mailman	come
minute	something	comb

EXERCISE B

The boldface words in the following phrases and sentences should be pronounced with [m]. Read them aloud as accurately as possible. **Remember, KEEP YOUR LIPS TOGETHER** (*especially when [m] is the last sound in the word*). **This exercise is not on the tape.**

1. **arm** in **arm**
2. **lemon** and **lime**
3. **summertime**
4. What's your **name**?
5. What **time** is it?
6. Don't **blame me**!
7. The **poem** doesn't **rhyme**.
8. **Sam** is a **common American name**.
9. What **time** is **my appointment**?
10. Tell **them** to **come home**.
11. **Tim** is **from** a **farm**.
12. Give **Pam some more ham**.
13. The **home team** won the **game**.
14. The picture **frame** is **made** of **chrome**.
15. **Mom makes homemade** ice **cream**.

Listen carefully to your teacher or the tape as five pairs of words are presented. **ONE** word in each pair is pronounced with [m]. Circle the number of the word with [m].

EXAMPLE: The instructor says: *some   sun*

You circle: ①   2

1. 1 2
2. 1 2
3. 1 2
4. 1 2
5. 1 2

PRONOUNCING [n]

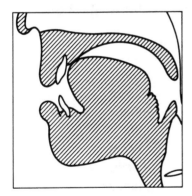

TONGUE: **is firmly pressed against gum ridge behind upper front teeth.**

AIRSTREAM: **is continuous through the nose.**

VOCAL CORDS: **are vibrating.**

SPANISH KEY WORDS WITH [n]

Spanish words with this sound are spelled with *n*.

KEY WORDS: *nada   uno   mano*

[m] as in ME, and [n] as in NO, and [ŋ] as in SING **137**

POSSIBLE PRONUNCIATION PROBLEMS
FOR THE SPANISH SPEAKER

Because of the similarity of the nasal consonants [m], [n], and [ŋ], Spanish speakers frequently confuse them in English, particularly at the end of words.

EXAMPLES: If you say [m] instead of [n]: **sun** will sound like **some**
If you say [ŋ] instead of [n]: **ran** will sound like **rang**

ALWAYS press your tongue tip firmly against the gum ridge behind your upper front teeth, *especially at the end of words.* **Practice this SOUND AGAIN and AGAIN; you'll have a FINE PRONUNCIATION of [n]!**

 # EXERCISE A

The following words should be pronounced with [n]. Repeat them after your teacher or the instructor on the tape. (**Remember—tongue tip up!**)

[n] At the Beginning	[n] In the Middle	[n] At the End
no	any	in
new	many	on
net	money	can
know	window	when
knee	banana	then
nail	dinner	fine
neck	tennis	begin
need	runner	again
night	candle	nineteen

NOTE ABOUT "SYLLABIC [n]": When an unstressed syllable begins with [t] or [d] and ends with [n], the [n] is frequently pronounced as "syllabic [n]." It is formed by keeping the tongue tip on the upper gum ridge without moving it from the position of the preceding [t] or [d].

EXAMPLES: *sadden kitten curtain beaten rotten sudden*

HINTS: 1. The letter *n* is almost always pronounced [n]. (Note the exception described in the following hint.)

2. When *n* follows *m* in the same syllable, it is usually NOT pronounced.

   EXAMPLES: *column   solemn   hymn   autumn*

EXERCISE B

The boldface words in the following phrases and sentences should be pronounced with [n]. Read them aloud carefully. ***Remember, tongue tip up*** (especially when [n] is the last sound in a word). **This exercise is not on the tape**.

1. **Answer** the **phone**.
2. Come **again**.
3. **rain** or **shine**
4. I **don't know**.
5. **Open** the **window**.
6. Leave me **alone**.

7. **Dinner** is **between seven and nine**.
8. **Dan** is a **fine man**.
9. The **brown pony** is **in** the **barn**.
10. **Ben** will be **on** the **ten** o'clock **train**.
11. Come **down when** you **can**.
12. **Everyone** has **fun in** the **sun**.
13. I **need** a **dozen lemons**.
14. **Turn on** the **oven** at **noon**.
15. **John** has a **broken bone**.

 **SELF-TEST I**   (Correct answers may be found in the Appendix on p. 215.)

Listen carefully to your teacher or the tape as 10 pairs of sentences are presented. Circle **S** if both sentences in the pair are the **SAME**. If they are **DIFFERENT**, circle **D**.

Sentence Pair Response

EXAMPLE A   S Ⓓ   (Is it **Tim**? It is **tin**?)

EXAMPLE B   Ⓢ D   (I feel **fine**. I feel **fine**.)

1. S D
2. S D
3. S D
4. S D
5. S D

PRONOUNCING [ŋ]

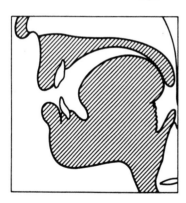

BACK OF TONGUE: is raised toward the soft palate.

AIRSTREAM: is continuous through the nose.

VOCAL CORDS: are vibrating.

The sound [ŋ] exists in Spanish when the letter *n* is followed by *g*, *c*, or *j* (*cangrejo*, *encantar*, *un juego*). In many dialects of Spanish, particularly in the Spanish of Cuba, the Dominican Republic, and Central America, *n* at the end of words is pronounced [ŋ] (*pan* = [paŋ]).

SPANISH KEY WORDS WITH [ŋ]

Spanish words have this sound when *n* is followed by *g, c,* or *j.*

KEY WORDS: *tengo   banco   monja*

POSSIBLE PRONUNCIATION PROBLEMS
FOR THE SPANISH SPEAKER

Many Spanish speakers are unaccustomed to pronouncing [ŋ] at the end of words. Also, the similarity between [ŋ] and [n] might confuse you.

EXAMPLES: If you say [n] instead of [ŋ]:   ***feeling*** will sound like ***feelin***
                                                          sing   will sound like ***sin***

The key to pronouncing [ŋ] correctly is to raise the **BACK** of your tongue— **NOT** the *TIP! Just keep STUDYING, THINKING, and PRACTICING; EVERYTHING will be OK with [ŋ]!!!*

EXERCISE A

The following words should be pronounced with [ŋ]. Repeat them carefully after your teacher or the instructor on the tape.

[ŋ] **In the Middle**	[ŋ] **At the End**
anger	rang
thank	sting
single	strong
hungry	belong
finger	tongue
banging	walking
ringing	feeling
longest	singing
youngest	running

EXERCISE B

Read the following phrases and sentences aloud carefully. The boldface words should be pronounced with [ŋ]. (*Remember—back of the tongue must go up toward the palate*). **This exercise is not on the tape.**

1. Good **evening**.
2. I'm **going** home.
3. Is **something wrong**?
4. **ring** on my **finger**
5. **raining** and **snowing**
6. Are you **coming along**?
7. The **singer sang** the **song**.
8. Mrs. **King** is **doing** the **washing**.
9. I **think** the **young** boy is **winning**.
10. We are **studying reading** and **writing**.
11. The **gang*** is **leaving** this **morning**.
12. **Bring** the **string** for the **fishing** rod.
13. We're **learning** the **English language**.
14. I'm **cooking string** beans this **evening**.
15. Are they **driving** to **Washington** this **spring**?

Gang = cuadrilla; banda.

 **SELF-TEST I**   (Correct answers may be found in the Appendix on p. 216.)

Listen carefully to your teacher or to the tape as five pairs of sentences are presented. **ONE** sentence in each pair will have a word pronounced with [ŋ]. Circle the number of the sentence with the [ŋ] word.

EXAMPLE: The instructor says: *He's a **swinger**.*   *He's a **swimmer**.*

You circle: ①   2

1. 1 2
2. 1 2
3. 1 2
4. 1 2
5. 1 2

 **SELF-TEST II**   (Correct answers may be found in the Appendix on p. 216.)

Listen carefully to your teacher or to the tape as the following words are presented. Circle only the words that are pronounced with [ŋ].

1. bring
2. anger
3. hang
4. angel
5. dancing
6. tangerine
7. swing
8. tangle
9. danger
10. sink
11. along
12. talking
13. sponge
14. grin
15. running
16. engage
17. stinging
18. stingy
19. lunch
20. bank

```
**********************************************
```

REVIEW

[m] [n] [ŋ]

```
**********************************************
```

 **ORAL EXERCISE**

Repeat the rows of words and sentences accurately after your teacher or the instructor on the tape. Feel the movement from the **lips—tongue tip—back of throat** as you pronounce [m]—[n]—[ŋ].

[m]	[n]	[ŋ]
1. whi**m**	wi**n**	wi**ng**
2. so**me**	su**n**	su**ng**
3. ru**m**	ru**n**	ru**ng**
4. ra**m**	ra**n**	ra**ng**
5. Ki**m**	ki**n**	ki**ng**
6. Is that a **clam**?	Is that a **clan**?	Is that a **clang**?
7. He is **Kim**.	He is **kin**.	He is **king**.
8. The **bam** was sudden.	The **ban** was sudden.	The **bang** was sudden.
9. They had **rum**.	They had **run**.	They had **rung**.
10. It was a **whim**.	It was a **win**.	It was a **wing**.

11. My **son sang some songs**.
     [n] [ŋ]   [m]   [ŋ]

12. **Tim thinks** that **thing** is **thin**.
     [m] [ŋ]   [ŋ]   [n]

13. **Kim** is **kin** to the **king**.
     [m]   [n]   [ŋ]

14. It's a **whim** to **win** the **wings**.
       [m]   [n]   [ŋ]

15. I **seem** to have **seen** him **sing**.
     [m]   [n]   [ŋ]

SELF-TEST I (Correct answers may be found in the Appendix on p. 216.)

Your teacher or the instructor on the tape will say only **ONE** word in each of the following pairs. Listen carefully and circle the word you hear.

EXAMPLES: A. sing   (sin)

B. (foam)   phone

1. thin	thing	6. seem	scene
2. ban	bang	7. some	sung
3. sinner	singer	8. hammer	hanger
4. comb	cone	9. ram	rang
5. rum	run	10. gone	gong

SELF-TEST II (Correct answers may be found in the Appendix on p. 216.)

Read the following sentences aloud; choose the correct word to complete the sentence. Be sure to pronounce each nasal consonant carefully. **This self-test is not on the tape.**

Pronunciation Hints: [m] = lips together.
[n] = tongue tip to upper gum ridge.
[ŋ] = back of tongue up to soft palate.

1. Jean sat in the _____.   (sum   sun   sung)
2. The bird hurt his _____.   (whim   win   wing)
3. It is fun to _____.   (rum   run   rung)
4. The meat needs to _____.   (simmer   sinner   singer)
5. They removed the _____.   (bam   ban   band)

SELF-TEST III

(Correct answers may be found in the Appendix on p. 217.)

Your teacher or the instructor on the tape will present the following sentences using ONLY ONE of the choices. Listen carefully and circle the word and consonant used.

EXAMPLE: Give me the (cone   (comb).
              [n]   [m]

1. I'll call (them   then).
            [m]   [n]
2. He (ran   rang) twice.
       [n]   [ŋ]
3. That (bun   bum) is old.
         [n]   [m]
4. We got (some   sun) at the beach.
           [m]   [n]
5. I heard a (bam   bang).
              [m]   [ŋ]
6. You shouldn't (sing   sin).
                  [ŋ]   [n]
7. The children like (swinging   swimming).
                      [ŋ]   [m]
8. It's a small (ping   pin).
                 [ŋ]   [n]
9. Get rid of the (gum   gun).
                   [m]   [n]
10. Buy another (hammer   hanger).
                 [m]   [ŋ]

After checking your answers in the Appendix, read each of the sentences twice. Use the first word in the first reading and the contrast word in the second reading.

SELF-TEST IV

(Correct answers may be found in the Appendix on p. 217.)

Read the following "commercial" aloud. In the brackets provided, write the phonetic symbol representing the sound of the underlined letters. **This self-test is not on the tape.**

Pronunciation Key: [m] as in *me*
[n] as in *no*
[ŋ] as in *ring*

. . . .

ANNOUNCER: Is your ski<u>n</u> feeli<u>ng</u> dry? Are you findi<u>ng</u> new wri<u>n</u>kles and
[n] [ŋ] [ ] [ ]
li<u>n</u>es? The<u>n</u> you <u>n</u>eed Po<u>m</u>'s Ski<u>n</u> Crea<u>m</u>. Me<u>n</u> and wome<u>n</u>
[ ] [ ] [ ] [ ] [ ] [ ]
everywhere are talki<u>ng</u> about our crea<u>m</u>. Liste<u>n</u> to fa-
[ ] [ ] [ ] [ ]
mous fil<u>m</u>star <u>M</u>olly <u>M</u>alo<u>n</u>e who has bee<u>n</u> acti<u>ng</u> for a
[ ] [ ] [ ] [ ]
lo<u>ng</u>, lo<u>ng</u>, lo<u>ng</u> time.
[ ] [ ] [ ]

MOLLY: Hmmmmm. Of course, everyo<u>n</u>e <u>kn</u>ows I started maki<u>ng</u>
[ ] [ ] [ ] [ ] [ ]
fil<u>m</u>s whe<u>n</u> I was ni<u>n</u>e. But I've bee<u>n</u> usi<u>ng</u> Po<u>m</u>'s Crea<u>m</u>
[ ] [ ] [ ] [ ]
for years and I thi<u>n</u>k it's wo<u>n</u>derful. Just put it on every
[ ] [ ] [ ] [ ]
mor<u>n</u>i<u>ng</u> and eve<u>n</u>i<u>ng</u> and i<u>n</u> one week you'll start seei<u>ng</u>
[ ] [ ] [ ]
the difference. Your face will glea<u>m</u> and shi<u>n</u>e and you'll
[ ]
look just fi<u>n</u>e!

ANNOUNCER: And now for a li<u>m</u>ited ti<u>m</u>e, you ca<u>n</u> get two jars for
[ ] [ ] [ ] [ ]
the price of o<u>n</u>e. Re<u>m</u>e<u>m</u>ber, use Po<u>m</u>'s Ski<u>n</u> Crea<u>m</u> and
[ ] [ ] [ ] [ ] [ ]
you too can look like a fil<u>m</u> star!
[ ]

. . . .

****

GENERAL REVIEW ACTIVITIES

****

THE GENERAL REVIEW ACTIVITIES IN THIS SECTION ARE DESIGNED TO ASSESS THE SKILLS YOU HAVE DEVELOPED.
They also serve as more material to help you practice the consonant sounds you have learned.

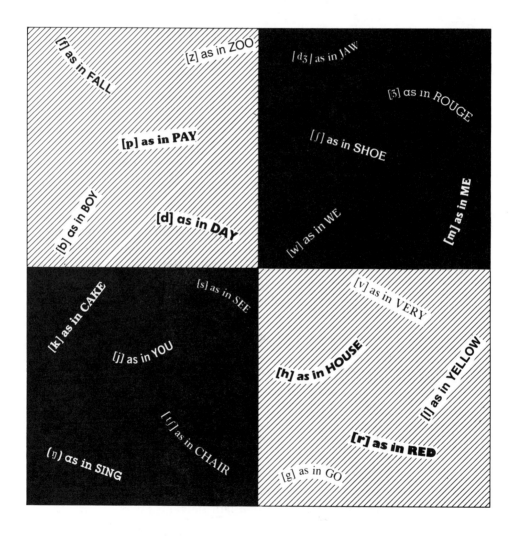

GENERAL REVIEW ACTIVITY I

(Correct answers may be found in the Appendix on p. 218.)

Repeat the following groups of rhyming words after your teacher or instructor on the tape. Fill in the blank with a word that rhymes with the others. In the brackets to the right of each blank, write the phonetic symbol representing the final sound of the words in each series.

EXAMPLE: dash   sash   rash   <u>cash</u>   [ʃ]

1.	nice	rice	twice	_____	[ ]
2.	math	path	wrath	_____	[ ]
3.	trees	knees	seas	_____	[ ]
4.	patch	hatch	batch	_____	[ ]
5.	puff	rough	cuff	_____	[ ]
6.	age	wage	stage	_____	[ ]
7.	glove	of	dove	_____	[ ]
8.	baking	shaking	making	_____	[ ]
9.	home	comb	foam	_____	[ ]
10.	blessed	test	zest	_____	[ ]

GENERAL REVIEW ACTIVITY II

(Correct answers may be found in the Appendix on p. 218.)

Listen carefully to your teacher or to the tape as 10 groups of three words are presented. Circle the phonetic symbol that identifies the sound each group of words has in common.

EXAMPLE: The instructor says: *wished*   *fast*   *talked*

You circle: [s]   [w]   ⟨[t]⟩

1. [s]   [z]   [θ]   6. [ʤ]   [j]   [ʒ]
2. [ð]   [d]   [t]   7. [p]   [b]   [v]
3. [ʃ]   [tʃ]   [ʤ]   8. [b]   [v]   [f]
4. [ʃ]   [j]   [s]   9. [m]   [n]   [ŋ]
5. [ʤ]   [j]   [ŋ]   10. [m]   [n]   [ŋ]

GENERAL REVIEW ACTIVITY III

(Correct answers may be found in the Appendix on p. 218.)

Read the following sentences aloud. Circle the phonetic symbol that represents the sound of the boldface letters. **This review activity is not on the tape.**

EXAMPLE: The flight **l**eft Ho**ll**and at twe**l**ve noon.   [r]   (**[l]**)   [w]

1. The bee**s** are bu**s**y bu**zz**ing in the flower**s**.   [s]   [z]   [ð]
2. Nei**th**er fa**th**er nor mo**th**er have a bro**th**er.   [θ]   [ð]   [d]
3. They are eati**ng** and drinki**ng** everythi**ng**.   [n]   [g]   [ŋ]
4. The tea**ch**er **ch**ose a mature **ch**ild.   [ʃ]   [tʃ]   [t]
5. My ne**ph**ew Frank is a **f**ine **ph**otogra**ph**er.   [v]   [f]   [p]

GENERAL REVIEW ACTIVITY IV

(Correct answers may be found in the Appendix on p. 219.)

Read the following joke aloud. In the brackets above the words, write the phonetic symbol representing the sound of the boldface letter(s). (Use the **Key to Pronouncing the Consonants of American English** on page 8 as necessary.) **This review activity is not on the tape.**

....

[tʃ]
An After-Dinner Spee**ch**

[ ]   [ ]   [ ]
A **Y**ale University gra**du**ate was ask**ed** to speak at a dinner. He
[ ]   [ ]   [ ]
deci**d**ed to speak about Yale. He said, "Yale, Y A L E. **Th**e Y stand**s** for
[ ]   [ ]   [ ] [ ]   [ ]
youth." He tal**k**ed about **y**ou**th** for **h**alf an hour. **Th**en he said, "The A stands
[ ]   [ ]   [ ][ ]
for am**b**ition." He talked about ambition for an unu**s**ually lo**ng** **t**ime.

[ ]   [ ] [ ]   [ ]

The Yale **g**raduate then said, "The L repre**s**ents **l**oyalty." He spo**k**e

                [ ]   [ ]   [ ]

about loyalty for almost an hour. **F**inally he reach**ed** E; he said "E stand**s** for

  [ ] [ ]

effi**ci**en**c**y."

                      [ ] [ ]   [ ]   [ ]

After he talked abou**t** e**ffi**ciency for a long **ti**me he sat down. **O**ne

           [ ]   [ ]   [ ]   [ ]   [ ] [ ]   [ ] [ ]

man in the audien**c**e ask**ed** ano**th**er man, "**Wh**at do **y**ou **th**ink o**f** hi**s**

  [ ]   [ ]   [ ]   [ ]   [ ]

spee**ch**?" The man replied, "I'm **th**ankful **th**at he didn't gra**d**uate from the

  [ ]   [ ]   [ ] [ ]

Massa**ch**usetts Institute of Te**ch**nolo**gy**!"

....

After checking your answers in the Appendix, practice telling this joke to at least three different people.

****

PRONOUNCING FINAL CONSONANT SOUNDS

****

FINAL CONSONANTS IN ENGLISH

A final consonant is any consonant that is the last sound in a word. Consonant sounds that end words are *very* important. They can determine grammatical as well as word meaning. Careful production of final consonants is necessary to convey your message correctly and to sound like a native English speaker.

> **NOTE: Words pronounced with a final consonant often have "*e*" as the final letter. When "*e*" is the last letter in a word, it is usually silent; a consonant is actually the last SOUND.**
>
> EXAMPLES: *made   phone   bite   have*

POSSIBLE PRONUNCIATION PROBLEMS FOR THE SPANISH SPEAKER

In Spanish, the majority of words end in vowels. In fact, most Spanish consonants are NEVER found at the end of words. The opposite is true in English. The majority of words end in consonants. Because you are not used to using final consonants in Spanish, you frequently omit them at the end of words in English. Without realizing it, you can confuse your listeners, and they will have trouble understanding you.

EXAMPLE 1:   Your grammar will sound incorrect:

    A. Past tense verbs will sound like present tense verbs:

        stayed will sound like **stay**
        raced will sound like **race**

    B. Plural nouns will sound like singular nouns:

        cars will sound like **car**
        hats will sound like **hat**

EXAMPLE 2: You will not be saying your target word:

place will sound like *play*
card will sound like *car*

EXAMPLE 3: Your listener won't understand you at all:

Ca without a final consonant is meaningless. You could be trying to say *case*, *came*, *cake*, *cane*, *cage*, *cape*, or *cave*. Your listener would have to guess!

EXERCISE A

The words in each of the following rows will sound the same if their final consonant sound is omitted. Repeat each row after your teacher or the instructor on the tape. *Exaggerate* your pronunciation of the final consonant in each word.

1. cat	cap	can	cab
2. bowl	bowls	bold	bolt
3. rag	rat	rap	rack
4. coal	colt	cold	coals
5. wrote	robe	rode	rope
6. soon	soup	suit	sued
7. ten	tense	tent	tend
8. sight	side	sign	size
9. bill	bills	build	built
10. cord	corn	court	cork

EXERCISE B

Read the following phrases aloud. Carefully distinguish between the phrases in each row by **exaggerating** your pronunciation of the final consonants. **This exercise is not on the tape**.

1. I saw.	eye sore	I sawed.
2. Joe knows her.	Joan knows her.	Joan owes her.
3. heat wave	He waved.	He waves.
4. I'll earn it.	I learn it.	I earn it.
5. I sigh.	eye sight	I sighed.

EXERCISE C

Read the following sentences aloud. **Exaggerate** your pronunciation of the final consonant sound in each boldface word. **This exercise is not on the tape**.

1. She **sighed** at the beautiful **sight**.
2. **Bess** is the **best** artist.
3. **Can't** Amy **catch** a **cab**?
4. The thief **stole** the **stove**.
5. **Ben** couldn't **bend** his knees.
6. The **coal** is very **cold**.
7. We **paid** for the **pane** of glass.
8. **I'm** sure **I'll** go.
9. **Would** he like a **wool** coat?
10. She **sat** on the **sack** full of **sap**.

EXERCISE D

Read the following dialogue aloud. Be sure to **exaggerate** your pronunciation of the final consonant sound in each boldface word. **This exercise is not on the tape**.

. . . .

PATRICK: Hi, **Pam**. **Have** you **had** dinner at the **Old Inn**?
PAM: No, **Pat**. But **Bea** said their **beef** can't be **beat**.
PATRICK: And **Hal** told me to **have** the **ham**.
PAM: **Doug** said the **duck** was **done** just **right**.
PATRICK: And **Sue** thought the **soup** would **suit** a king!
PAM: **Kate raved** about the **cake**.
PATRICK: I'd say the **inn** was **it**! **Pam**, will you be ready at **eight**?
PAM: Oh, **Pat** I already **am**! I thought you'd never **ask**!!

. . . .

(The exciting story of **Pam** and **Pat** at the **Old Inn** continues in Self-Test IV.)

 SELF-TEST I   (Correct answers may be found in the Appendix on p. 219.)

Your teacher or the instructor on the tape will present 10 three-word series. Write the numbers 1, 2 or 3 on the line above each word to correspond with the order of word presentation. **Listen carefully** for the final consonant sound in each word.

EXAMPLE: The instructor says: *half*   *hat*   *had*

                                       2   3   1
                    You write: hat   had   half

1. ‾hot‾   ‾hog‾   ‾hop‾

2. ‾wrote‾   ‾rope‾   ‾robe‾

3. ‾save‾   ‾safe‾   ‾same‾

4. ‾big‾   ‾bid‾   ‾bib‾

5. right   ride   ripe

6. mad   mat   map

7. fade   fate   fake

8. wipe   white   wife

9. peg   pen   pet

10. prize   prime   pride

SELF-TEST II   (Correct answers may be found in the Appendix on p. 219.)

Read the following sentences aloud. **Exaggerate** the pronunciation of the final consonant sound of each word you choose to fill in the blanks. **This self-test is not on the tape.**

1. The key opens the _____.	(lock	log	lot)
2. The _____ is in the fire.	(lock	log	lot)
3. _____ the dirty dishes.	(Soak	Soap	Sole)
4. Wash your hands with _____.	(soak	soap	sole)
5. He _____ the letter.	(wrote	rose	rode)
6. He _____ the bicycle.	(wrote	rose	rode)
7. The _____ landed.	(plague	plane	plate)
8. The _____ is broken.	(plague	plane	plate)
9. Send a birthday _____.	(cart	card	carve)
10. The bags are in the _____.	(cart	card	carve)

SELF-TEST III

(Correct answers may be found in the Appendix on p. 220.)

Your teacher or instructor on the tape will present the following sentences using only **ONE** of the words in parentheses. Listen carefully for the final consonant sound and circle the word used.

EXAMPLE: The (cab (cat)) is lost.

1. I can't find the (belt   bell).
2. My son is (five   fine).
3. I think he's (dead   deaf).
4. Tim bought another (car   card).
5. The (guild   guilt) is ours.
6. The (pack   pact) was sealed.
7. There's a (lake   lane) near the house.
8. I (can   can't) go.
9. The (den   dent) is very small.
10. The (coal   colt) is black.

After checking your answers in the Appendix, read each of the sentences aloud twice. Use the first word in parentheses in the first reading and the contrast word in the second reading. **Exaggerate your pronunciation of final consonant sounds.**

SELF-TEST IV

(Correct answers may be found in the Appendix on p. 220.)

Read the following dialogue aloud. Fill in the blanks with the final consonant sound that completes the word. **This self-test is not on the tape.**

. . . .

ANN: Hi, **Pam**! How was your **da__e** last **nigh__** with **Pat**?
PAM: Nothing went **righ__** last **nigh__**. **Pa__** had a **fla__** tire and came **la__e**!
ANN: How was the **foo__** at the **Ol__ Inn**?
PAM: It was **ba__**. The soup was **col__**. My **stea__** was tough. They ran out of **chocola__e ca__e**.
ANN: What about the dinner **Pa__ a__e**?

PAM: His **duc__** was over**do__e**. His **garli__ brea__** was **sta__e**!
ANN: Did it **cos__** a lot of money?
PAM: Yes! and **Pat** didn't **ha__e** enough to pay the **bi__**.
ANN: I guess you **won'__** go **ou__** with him **agai__**!
PAM: Why do you say **tha__**? We're going for a bike **ri__e** this afternoon.
He's so **handso__e**!

. . . .

After checking your answers in the Appendix, practice this dialogue again.
Exaggerate your pronunciation of all final consonant sounds.

FOR AN ENCORE . . .

Tape-record yourself while talking on the telephone. After you hang up, play
the recording back. Analyze your speech and listen for final consonants. Make
a list of words you didn't pronounce carefully and practice them.

PRONOUNCING PAST TENSE VERBS

When writing English, we add the ending *-ed* to form the past tense of regular verbs. That's easy to remember! However, when **speaking** English, the *-ed* ending can have three different pronunciations. Sometimes *-ed* sounds like [t], as in *stopped* [stɑpt]; sometimes it sounds like [d], as in *lived* [lɪvd]; sometimes it sounds like a new syllable, [ɪd], as in *loaded* [loʊdɪd].

POSSIBLE PRONUNCIATION PROBLEMS
FOR THE SPANISH SPEAKER

As discussed in the chapter on final consonant sounds (page 152), most consonants are never found at the end of words in Spanish. Consequently, you are not used to saying final consonants in English. This might make you omit or mispronounce past tense verb endings.

EXAMPLE 1:   Past tense verbs will sound like present tense verbs:
washed will sound like **wash**
played will sound like **play**

EXAMPLE 2:   A new syllable will be incorrectly added to a past tense verb:
lived   [lɪvd] will sound like **live-id** [lɪvɪd]
tapped [tæpt] will sound like **tap-id** [tæpɪd]

EXAMPLE 3:   You will not be saying your target past tense verb:
played [pleɪd] will sound like **plate** [pleɪt]
tied   [tɑɪd] will sound like **tight** [tɑɪt]

This might seem confusing **but don't worry**! **WE HAVE GOOD NEWS**! In this chapter we will teach you three **EASY** rules to help you pronounce past tense regular verbs correctly. You will learn when *-ed* sounds like [t], [d], or [ɪd]. Study the rules and **you've got it made!**

-ed PRONOUNCED [t]

The ending -ed will always sound like [t] when the last sound in the present tense verb* is voiceless.†

EXAMPLES: *talked* [tɔkt]   *crossed* [krɔst]   *laughed* [læft]

 **EXERCISE A**

Repeat the following verbs after your teacher or the instructor on the tape. Be sure to pronounce the -ed in the past tense verbs like [t]. (Do NOT add a new syllable to any word!)

Present Tense Verbs	Past Tense Verbs
(Last sound is voiceless.)	**(-ed = [t].)**
1. look	looked
2. miss	missed
3. stop	stopped
4. work	worked
5. pick	picked
6. wash	washed
7. drip	dripped
8. pass	passed
9. place	placed
10. laugh	laughed

-ed PRONOUNCED [d]

The ending -ed will always sound like [d] when the last sound in the present tense verb is a vowel or voiced consonant.

EXAMPLES: *lived* [lɪvd]   *turned* [tɝnd]   *played* [pleɪd]

*Rules apply to *regular* past tense verbs.

† Refer to page 10 for a review of voiceless and voiced sounds.

EXERCISE B

Repeat the following verbs after your teacher or the instructor on the tape. Be sure to pronounce -ed like [d]. (Do NOT add a new syllable to the words!)

Present Tense Verbs	Past Tense Verbs
(Last sound is voiced.)	**(-ed = [d].)**
1. love	loved
2. stay	stayed
3. fill	filled
4. burn	burned
5. rain	rained
6. live	lived
7. clean	cleaned
8. stare	stared
9. study	studied
10. follow	followed

-ed PRONOUNCED [ɪd]

The ending -ed will always sound like the new syllable [ɪd] when the last sound in the present tense verb is [t] or [d].

EXAMPLES: *wanted* [wɑntɪd]   *rested* [rɛstɪd]   *ended* [ɛndɪd]

EXERCISE C

Repeat the following verbs after your teacher or the instructor on the tape. **NOW** you should pronounce -ed like the new syllable [ɪd]!

Present Tense Verbs	Past Tense Verbs
(End in *t* or *d*.)	**(-ed = the new syllable [ɪd].)**
1. end	ended
2. add	added
3. hunt	hunted
4. want	wanted

5. need	needed
6. fold	folded
7. start	started
8. print	printed
9. sound	sounded

EXERCISE D

Read the following sentences aloud. Be sure to pronounce the *-ed* ending in the past tense verbs correctly. **This exercise is not on the tape**.

-ed = [t]   **-ed** = [d]   **-ed** = [ɪd]

She cooked dinner.	We played a game.	He avoided his boss.
The boy danced all night.	He moved again.	I rested at home.
The bus stopped in the road.	Ted stayed out late.	The car started.
Mom baked a pie.	I mailed a letter.	Mike needed money.
She finished early.	We opened a window.	Our house was painted.

Sue packed her suitcase and waited for a taxi.
      [t]   [ɪd]
Tim cashed a check and deposited the money.
      [t]   [ɪd]
The children played games and jumped rope.
         [d]   [t]
I studied hard but failed the test.
  [d]   [d]
He listened while I showed photos and talked about my trip.
    [d]   [d]   [t]

 **SELF-TEST I**   (Correct answers may be found in the Appendix on p. 221.)

Your teacher or the instructor on the tape will present the following sentences using ONE of the words in parentheses. Listen carefully and circle the verb you hear.

EXAMPLE: They (start   (started)) school in September.

1. We   (live   lived)   in Spain.
2. The stores (open   opened) on Monday.
3. The farmers (plant planted) corn.
4. We   (talk   talked)   about our problems.
5. The banks   (loan   loaned) money.

SELF-TEST II   (Correct answers may be found in the Appendix on p. 221.)

Read the following sentences aloud. Choose the correct past tense verb from the list to fill in the blanks. In the brackets, write either [t], [d], or [ɪd] to represent the -ed sound in the verb. **This self-test is not on the tape**.

painted	mailed	danced	washed	waited
lived	deposited	asked	walked	talked

EXAMPLE: I locked the door. [t]

1. We _____ the rumba and tango. [ ]
2. She _____ on the phone for an hour. [ ]
3. Dad _____ the fence green. [ ]
4. The student _____ three questions. [ ]
5. They _____ 15 minutes for the bus. [ ]
6. I've _____ in the same house for four years. [ ]
7. My father _____ a letter. [ ]
8. The man _____ five miles. [ ]
9. I _____ my check in the bank. [ ]
10. He _____ his car with a hose. [ ]

SELF-TEST III   (Correct answers may be found in the Appendix on p. 221.)

Listen carefully to your teacher or the tape as five sentences are presented. Some of the -ed verb endings will be said **INCORRECTLY**. Circle C for "Correct" or I for "Incorrect" to indicate whether the past tense verb in each sentence is pronounced properly.

Sentence	Response	
EXAMPLE A:	C (I)	(She *baked* [beɪkɪd] a pie.)
EXAMPLE B:	(C) I	(I *liked* [laɪkt] the book.)
1.	C I	
2.	C I	
3.	C I	
4.	C I	
5.	C I	

SELF-TEST IV

(Correct answers may be found in the Appendix on p. 221.)

Repeat each 3-word series after your teacher or instructor on the tape. Circle the ONE word in each group that has a different *-ed* sound than the others.

EXAMPLE: (placed)   pleased   played

1.	stopped	started	stated
2.	finished	followed	phoned
3.	loved	looked	liked
4.	tasted	traded	taped
5.	cooked	cleaned	baked
6.	packed	pasted	passed
7.	ironed	sewed	mended
8.	whispered	shouted	screamed
9.	skipped	hopped	lifted
10.	pushed	pulled	raised

After checking your answers in the Appendix, practice reading the verbs aloud one more time.

Read the following dialogue aloud. In the brackets above each past tense verb, write the phonetic symbol representing the sound of the *-ed* ending. **This self-test is not on the tape.**

. . . .

                              [ɪd]
ROBERTA: Juanita, have you started your diet? I hope you haven't
                   [d]
            gained any weight.
                    [ ]   [ ]
JUANITA: I boiled eggs and sliced celery for lunch.
                          [ ]
ROBERTA: Have you exercised at all?
                    [ ]   [ ]
JUANITA: I walked five miles and jogged in the park.
                        [ ]   [ ]
ROBERTA: Have you cleaned the house? Calories can be worked off!
                    [ ]   [ ]   [ ]
JUANITA: I washed and waxed the floors. I even painted the bathroom.
                      [ ]   [ ]
ROBERTA: Who baked this apple pie? Who cooked this ham?
                        [ ]   [ ]   [ ]
JUANITA: When I finished cleaning I was starved. I prepared this food for
            dinner.
                                                              [ ]
ROBERTA: Oh, no! I'll take this food home so you won't be tempted. I
                      [ ]
            really enjoyed being with you. Your diet is great!
                        [ ]   [ ]
JUANITA: What happened? Somehow, I missed out on all the fun.

. . . .

After checking your answers in the Appendix, read this dialogue aloud with a friend. Be sure to pronounce all past tense endings correctly.

****

PRONOUNCING PLURALS, THIRD-PERSON VERBS, POSSESSIVES, AND CONTRACTIONS

****

When writing English, the letter **s** at the end of words serves many different purposes. **S** is used to form plural nouns (hats, dogs); third-person present tense regular verbs (he likes; she eats); possessive nouns (my friend's house; the dog's collar), and contractions (it's late; he's here). As you can see, **s** is a very versatile letter in English. It is important to learn its many different "sounds"!

When **speaking** English, the -s ending can have three different pronunciations. It can sound like [s], as in *hats* [hæts]; [z], as in *tells* [tɛlz]; or as the new syllable [ɪz], as in *roses* [roʊzɪz].

POSSIBLE PRONUNCIATION PROBLEMS FOR THE SPANISH SPEAKER

Once again, a Spanish speaker's tendency to drop final consonants results in omissions or incorrect pronunciations of -s at the ends of words. This will make you difficult to understand and confuse your listeners.

EXAMPLE 1:   Plural nouns will sound like singular nouns:

> **Two books** will sound like **two book**.

EXAMPLE 2:   Third-person present tense verbs will be incorrect:

> **He eats**   will sound like **he eat**.
> **She sings** will sound like **she sing**.

EXAMPLE 3:   Possessives and contractions will be omitted:

> **Bob's house** will sound like **Bob house**.
> **He's right**   will sound like **he right**.

EXAMPLE 4: You will not be saying your target word:

My eyes will sound like **my ice**.
Sue sings will sound like **Sue sinks**.

You are probably wondering if there are any rules to help you correctly pronounce *s* in all these different situations. **The answer is YES!** In this chapter, you will learn how to pronounce **s** when it forms plurals, third-person present tense verbs, possessives, and contractions. Study the rules and listen to the tapes carefully. **You will soon notice a big improvement in your pronunciation!**

-S PRONOUNCED [s]

The -s forming the plural always sounds like [s] when the last sound in the singular noun is voiceless.

EXAMPLES: *hats* [hæts]   *lips* [lɪps]   *sticks* [stɪks]

The -s forming the third-person present always sounds like [s] when the last sound in the verb infinitive is voiceless.

EXAMPLES: *he likes* [laɪks]   *she talks* [tɔks]   *it floats* [floʊts]

The -s forming the possessive always sounds like [s] when the last sound in the noun is voiceless.

EXAMPLES: *Pat's* [pæts] *car*   the *book's* [bʊks] *binding*

The -s forming contractions always sounds like [s] when the last sound in the word being contracted is voiceless.

EXAMPLES: *It's* [ɪts] *true.*   *That's* [ðæts] *my house.*

 **EXERCISE A**

Repeat the following phrases after your teacher or the instructor on the tape.
-*S* will sound like [s]. (Do NOT add a new syllable to any word!)

Plural Noun Phrases	Third-Person Verb Phrases	Possessive/ Contraction Phrases
Bake the cakes.	He smokes too much.	the cat's milk
Wash the plates.	She sleeps late.	Ralph's friend
Stack the cups.	It tastes good.	The plant's leaves
Clean the pots.	My mother makes tea.	Let's eat now.
Darn the socks.	The dog eats.	What's wrong?
Feed the cats.	He jumps high.	It's time to go.

-*S* PRONOUNCED [z]

The -*s* forming the plural always sounds like [z] when the last sound in the singular noun is voiced.

EXAMPLES: *floors* [flɔrz]   *bags* [bægz]   *cars* [kɑrz]

The -*s* forming the third-person present always sounds like [z] when the last sound in the verb infinitive is voiced.

EXAMPLES: *He swims* [swɪmz].   *The bird flies* [flɑɪz].   *She sings* [sɪŋz].

The -*s* forming the possessive always sounds like [z] when the last sound in the noun is voiced.

EXAMPLES: *Tim's* [tɪmz] *house*   *my friend's* [frɛndz] *cat*

The -*s* forming a contraction always sounds like [z] when the last sound in the word being contracted is voiced.

EXAMPLES: *She's* [ʃiz] *my sister.*   *He's* [hiz] *leaving.*

 **EXERCISE B**

Repeat the following phrases after your teacher or the instructor on the tape. Remember, the -s ending must sound like [z].

Plural Noun Phrases	Third-Person Verb Phrases	Possessive/Contraction Phrases
Close your eyes.	He saves money.	Sue's pencil
Kill the fleas.	The man lives here.	the baby's milk
Sing the songs.	Dad reads books.	our teacher's desk
lost 30 pounds	The boy listens.	my friend's house
Open the letters.	It smells good.	Here's a pencil.
Buy some shoes.	She sees me.	There's a note.

-*S* (or -*es*) PRONOUNCED [ɪz]

The -s or -es forming the plural always sounds like the new syllable [ɪz] when the last sound in the singular noun is [s], [z], [ʃ], [tʃ], [ʤ], or [ʒ].

EXAMPLES: *wishes* [wɪʃɪz] *churches* [tʃɝtʃɪz] *places* [pleɪsɪz]

The -s or -es forming the third-person present always sounds like the new syllable [ɪz] when the last sound in the verb infinitive is [s], [z], [ʃ], [tʃ], [ʤ], or [ʒ].

EXAMPLES: *He watches* [watʃɪz]. *The bee buzzes* [bʌzɪz].

The -s or -es forming the possessive always sounds like the new syllable [ɪz] when the last sound in the noun is [s], [z], [ʃ], [tʃ], [ʤ], or [ʒ].

EXAMPLES: *the rose's* [roʊzɪz] *stem* *the church's* [tʃɝtʃɪz] *altar*

 **EXERCISE C**

Repeat the following phrases after your teacher or the instructor on the tape.
Now you should pronounce s like the new syllable [ɪz]!

Plural Noun Phrases	Third-Person Verb Phrases	Possessive Phrases
two new dresses	He wishes.	the church's steeple
Trim the hedges.	She watches him.	the witch's broom
Buy the watches.	He judges the contest.	Mr. Jones's pen
Win the prizes.	Mother washes clothes.	the mouse's cheese
in the cages	The bee buzzes.	the bus's tires

EXERCISE D

Read the following sentences aloud. Be sure to pronounce the s ending in
the plurals, verbs, possessives, and contractions correctly. **This exercise is
not on the tape.**

s = [s]	**s** = [z]	**s** = [ɪz]
He wants to leave.	Blow out the candles.	The speeches are boring.
My sister likes gum.	The hen laid eggs.	Please turn the pages.
I read many books.	Guns are dangerous.	Mary dances well.
Mother ironed shirts.	Here's some money.	I won many prizes.
Jack's not coming.	The girl's dress is old.	You have three choices.

Boys play cowboys and Indians and use toy guns and knives.
  [z]   [z]   [z]   [z]   [z]
The store sells watches, rings, bracelets, diamonds, and rubies.
      [z]   [ɪz] [z]   [s]   [z]   [z]
My sister's dresses, blouses, and shoes are new.
  [z]   [ɪz]   [ɪz]   [z]
Our teacher's favorite saying is "Where there's a will, there's a way."
    [z]   [z]   [z]
Tim's friend's house has lots of rooms with oriental carpets.
[z]   [z]   [s]   [z]   [s]

EXERCISE E

Read the following dialogue aloud with a friend or classmate. Be sure to pronounce all -s endings correctly. **This exercise is not on the tape.**

CHARLES: Hi, James. What's new?
           [z]   [s]

JAMES: Nothing Charles. All the guys have dates for the prom except
                   [z]   [z]   [s]
me!

CHARLES: That's all right. You can take Bess's sister Nancy.
        [s]   [ɪz]

JAMES: What's she like?
       [s]

CHARLES: She measures about 5 feet 2 inches, has blue eyes, and
          [z]   [ɪz]   [z]
weighs 102 pounds. She looks like a model.
 [z]   [z]   [s]

JAMES: Then she probably dislikes her studies.
                 [s]   [z]

CHARLES: That's not true. She enters law school after finals. She's on the
        [s]   [z]   [z] [z]
Dean's List.*
 [z]

JAMES: What are her hobbies? She probably hates sports!
            [z]   [s] [s]

CHARLES: She golfs, plays tennis, and swims. She also dances very well.
      [s] [z]   [z]   [ɪz]

JAMES: There's got to be SOMETHING wrong! She probably has no
     [z]
dates.
 [s]

CHARLES: She has lots of boyfriends. In fact, let's make some changes. I'll
      [s]   [z]   [s]   [ɪz]
take Bess's sister! You can take Mary.
 [ɪz]

JAMES: NO WAY! There will be no exchanges! Nancy sounds great. I
                        [ɪz]   [z]
just hope she likes me!
        [s]

*Dean's List = inscripto en la lista de distinción en la universidad.

SELF-TEST I   (Correct answers may be found in the Appendix on p. 222.)

Your teacher or the instructor on the tape will present the following sentences using ONE of the words in parentheses. Listen carefully and circle the word used.

EXAMPLE: Did you pay for the ((blouse) blouses)?

1. The men cut the (tree   trees).
2. He repaired the (watch   watches).
3. The (book   book's) cover is red.
4. Did they finally make (peace   peas)?
5. Did you see the little (cups   cubs)?

Now that you have completed the self-test, read each of the sentences twice. Pronounce the first word in parentheses the first time and the contrast word the second time.

SELF-TEST II   (Correct answers may be found in the Appendix on p. 222.)

Repeat each three-word series after your teacher or instructor on the tape. Circle the ONE word in each group of three that has a different -s ending sound than the others.

EXAMPLE: belts   hats   (ties)

1.	talks	walks	runs
2.	dishes	gates	pages
3.	pears	apples	oranges
4.	eyes	noses	toes
5.	saves	makes	cooks
6.	newspapers	magazines	books
7.	dogs	birds	cats
8.	tables	chairs	couches
9.	dentists	doctors	lawyers
10.	lunches	beaches	chimes

Read the following passages from William Shakespeare's plays aloud. Circle all words with -s suffixes and write them under the phonetic symbol representing the sound of their -s ending. **This self-test is not on the tape.**

....

(Passages) from (Shakespeare's) (Plays)

All the world's a stage,
And all the men and women merely players;
They have their exits and their entrances;
And one man in his time plays many parts,
His acts being seven ages.

(from *As You Like It*)

Good name in man and woman, dear my Lord,
Is the immediate jewel of their souls;
Who steals my purse steals trash; 'tis something, nothing
'Twas mine, 'tis his, and has been slave to thousands
But he that filches* from me my good name
Robs me of that which not enriches† him
And makes me poor indeed.

(from *Othello*)

Hath not a Jew eyes?
Hath not a Jew hands, organs, dimensions, senses, affections, passions?
Fed with the same food?
Hurt with the same weapons?
Subject to the same diseases?
Healed by the same means?
Warmed and cooled by the same winter and summer, as a Christian is?

from *The Merchant of Venice*

*Filches = ratear; hurtar.

† Enriches = enriquecer; adornar.

PLURALS, THIRD-PERSON VERBS, POSSESSIVES, AND CONTRACTIONS **173**

[s]	[z]	[ɪz]
	Shakespeare's plays	passages

THAT'S ALL FOLKS!

Believe it or not, you have just finished reading the LAST chapter in the book. **CONGRATULATIONS**! You've earned your degree in *English Pronunciation for Spanish Speakers: Consonants*. It was worth all that hard work, wasn't it? **But education is a continuing process.** *Although we've stressed it all along, we'll say it again:* **THE MORE YOU PRACTICE, THE BETTER YOU WILL BECOME**.

Daniel Webster once said, "*If all my possessions were taken from me with one exception, I would choose to keep the power of communication, for by it, I would soon regain all the rest.*"

SO—keep practicing, and CLEAR, EFFECTIVE COMMUNICATION WILL BE YOURS FOREVER.

Best of luck always,

Paulette Dale and Lillian Poms

****

TO THE TEACHER

****

WELCOME TO THE CHALLENGE! You recommended *English Pronunciation for Spanish Speakers* to your students because you are committed to helping them improve their pronunciation of English. This is a difficult task. But it's NOT impossible. Teaching and learning English pronunciation can be difficult and tedious work. They can also be more fun than you ever imagined possible! (In our accent reduction classes, there have been countless occasions when we, along with our students, have laughed long and hard enough for the tears to roll!)

Some of you are already experienced ESL or speech instructors and/or speech pathologists involved in teaching foreign accent reduction classes, and you already employ a variety of effective techniques when working with your students. PLEASE—share some of your most successful ones with us. And we invite you to let us know how you like OUR suggestions. **We truly look forward to hearing from you**!

Some of you are new at teaching English pronunciation to nonnative speakers. *DON'T WORRY!* An enthusiastic attitude and genuine desire to learn with your students will be more valuable than years of experience. As you'll quickly realize, the *English Pronunciation for Spanish Speakers* program provides you with an easy to follow, systematic approach to teaching English pronunciation.

BREAKING THE ICE

As previously mentioned, teaching foreign accent reduction can and should be fun for all concerned. At first students will invariably be apprehensive and self-conscious about taking such a course and "exposing" their speech patterns in front of you and their peers. The time you spend trying to alleviate their initial concerns will be time well spent. We recommend

1. Using the first class meeting to discuss "accents" in general. Elaborate on the information presented on page 2 of "To the Student."

2. Emphasizing that accent reduction is NOT the losing of one's culture or heritage but the improvement of a skill.

3. Describing your own embarrassing mistakes or those of other native Americans when speaking a foreign language. Our students are comforted by

the thought that we, too, have pronunciation difficulties when speaking our second language.

HEARING THE SOUNDS

Advise your students that their initial difficulty in hearing the various consonant sounds is perfectly normal. Nonnative speakers of English frequently have trouble recognizing sounds absent in their native language. Scholes* found that the sound system of one's native language will influence one's perception of English phonemes. Your students will overcome this initial "deafness" of specific sounds after directed auditory discrimination practice.

ACCENT ANALYSIS

The **Accent Analysis** should be used at the beginning of the *English Pronunciation for Spanish Speakers* program. Record each student (or have them record themselves at home) reading the **Accent Analysis Sentences**. Each pair is designed to survey the students' pronunciation of a specific target consonant. Encourage them to read the sentences in a natural, conversational voice. The accent analysis should be used again when your students complete the program. This will help you (and them) measure their progress.

Now you are ready to listen to your students' tapes and do a written survey of their pronunciation difficulties with consonants, past tense verbs, and plural nouns. The **Summary of Errors** form on page 183 provides a place to record the results. The pairs of **Accent Analysis Sentences** are numbered to correspond with the phonetic symbols.

As each group of sentences is read, listen only to the pronunciation of the target consonant. Ignore all other errors. While a student is reading, follow along sentence by sentence on the **Teacher's Record Form**. Circle all target words that are mispronounced. On the line above the mispronounced target word, record the error. Use any marking (e.g., phonetic) which is meaningful to you. You can then complete the **Summary of Errors** form on page 183 at your leisure.

*Scholes, R. "Phonetic Interference as a Perceptual Phenomenon," *Language and Speech*, 11, 86–103, 1968.

EXAMPLE: Your student substitutes [s] (as in *sit*) and [t] (as in *to*) for [θ] in sentence 5, target words *think*, *nothing*, and *threat*, *third*, respectively. You might record the errors as follows:

                     [t]   [t]

[θ] 5.   Is there a **threat**? of World War **Three**? After a **third** war, many

  [s]   [s]

think there will be **nothing** left on **earth**. We must be **thankful** for peace.

On the **Summary of Errors** form, you might note the following:

CONSONANTS	Correct	Error	Comments
5. [θ] as in *think*	_____	[s] & [t] for [θ]	errors are inconsistent

ACCENT ANALYSIS SENTENCES

1. The United States started with 13 small states. Now there are 50 states spread from east to west.

2. Lazy cows graze in the fields of New Zealand. The pleasant breeze blows from the seas.

3. *A Tale of Two Cities* was written by Charles Dickens. Today it is taught throughout the world.

4. Dad had a bad cold. He stayed in bed all day Monday and Tuesday .

5. Is there a threat of World War Three? After a third war, many think there will be nothing left on earth. We must be thankful for peace.

6. My mother and father loathe northern weather. They prefer the climate of the southern states.

7. Sherry took a short vacation to Washington. She went fishing and found shells along the ocean shore.

8. China has a culture which changes every year. But the Chinese teachings and rituals are very charming.

9. I made a decision to paint the garage beige. I usually paint or watch television in my leisure time.

10. George is majoring in education. He will graduate from college next June.

11. Year after year, millions of people visit New York. Young and old enjoy familiar sights.

12. Pick up a pack of ripe apples. Mom will bake apple pie for supper.

13. Bob built a big boat. He finds lobster and crab and cooks them in the cabin below.

14. The elephant is friendly and full of life. It's a fact that an elephant never forgets!

15. Leave the veal and gravy in the oven. Vicky wants to keep it very hot. She will serve everyone at seven.

16. Kathy can't bake a cake for the card party. She is working at the bank until six o'clock.

17. Gambling is legal in Las Vegas. Gamblers go for the big win!

18. We would like to see the Seven Wonders of the World. We will just have to wait awhile!

19. Roads are rough in rural areas. Be very careful when you drive your car.

20. Bolivar became a military and political leader. He was truly the liberator of Latin America.

21. Heaven helps those who help themselves. Anyhow, hard work never hurt anyone.

22. I'm coming home for Christmas. As the poem says, "Wherever you may roam, there's no place like home."

23. Now you can learn to pronounce the consonants. Practice them again and again on your own.

24. The strong young men are exercising this morning. They are running long distances.

25. Mother washed, cooked, and cleaned. After she finished, she rested.

26. Put the shoes and boots in the boxes. Hang the dresses and pants on the hangers.

. . . .

TARGET CONSONANTS

[s]   1. The United **States started** with 13 **small states**. Now there are 50 **states spread** from **east** to **west**.

[z]   2. **Lazy cows graze** in the **fields** of New **Zealand**. The **pleasant breeze blows** from the **seas**.

[t]   3. A **Tale** of **Two Cities** was **written** by Charles Dickens. **Today it** is **taught throughout** the world.

[d]   4. **Dad had** a **bad cold**. He **stayed** in **bed** all **day Monday and Tuesday**.

[θ]   5. Is there a **threat** of World War **Three**? After a **third** war, many **think** there will be **nothing** left on **earth**. We must be **thankful** for peace.

[ð]   6. My **mother** and **father loathe northern weather**. **They** prefer **the** climate of **the southern** states.

[ʃ]   7. **Sherry** took a **short vacation** to **Washington**. **She** went **fishing** and found **shells** along the **ocean shore**.

[tʃ]   8. **China** has a **culture which changes each** year. But the **Chinese teachings** and **rituals** are very **charming**.

[ʒ]   9. I made a **decision** to paint the **garage beige**. I **usually** paint or watch **television** in my **leisure** time.

[ʤ]   10. **George** is **majoring** in **education**. He will **graduate** from **college** next **June**.

[j] 11. **Year** after **year, millions** of people visit New **York. Young** and old enjoy **familiar** sights.

[p] 12. **Pick up** a **pack** of **ripe apples.** Mom will bake **apple pie** for **supper**.

[b] 13. **Bob built** a **big boat.** He finds **lobster** and **crab** and cooks them in the **cabin below.**

[f] 14. The **elephant** is **friendly** and **full** of **life.** It's a **fact** that an **elephant** never **forgets**!

[v] 15. **Leave** the **veal** and **gravy** in the **oven. Vicky** wants to keep it **very** hot. She will **serve everyone** at **seven.**

[k] 16. **Kathy can't bake** a **cake** for the **card** party. She is **working** at the **bank** until six **o'clock.**

[g] 17. **Gambling** is **legal** in Las **Vegas. Gamblers go** for the **big** win!

[w] 18. **We would** like to see the Seven **Wonders** of the **World. We will** just have to **wait awhile!**

[r] 19. **Roads are rough** in **rural areas.** Be **very careful** when you **drive your car.**

[l] 20. **Bolivar** became a **military** and **political leader.** He was **truly** the **liberator** of **Latin** America.

[h] 21. **Heaven helps** those **who help** themselves. **Anyhow, hard** work never **hurt** anyone.

[m] 22. **I'm coming home** for **Christmas.** As the **poem** says, "Wher-ever you **may roam,** there's no place like **home.**"

[n]   23. **Now** you **can learn** to **pronounce** the **consonants**. Practice
       them **again and again on** your **own**.

[ŋ]   24. The **strong young** men are **exercising** this **morning**. They are
       running long distances.

Past Tense

25. Mother wash**ed**, cook**ed**, and clean**ed**.
         [t]   [t]   [d]

   After she finish**ed**, she rest**ed**
            [t]   [ɪd]

Plurals

26. Put the shoe**s** and boot**s** in the box**es**. Hang the dress**es** and pant**s** on
         [z]   [s]   [ɪz]   [ɪz]   [s]

   the hanger**s**.
         [z]

Student's Name: _____   Date: _____

Summary of Errors

Correct	Error		Comments

CONSONANTS

1. [s] as in *see* _____ _____ for [s] _____
2. [z] as in *zoo* _____ _____ for [z] _____
3. [t] as in *too* _____ _____ for [t] _____
4. [d] as in *dog* _____ _____ for [d] _____
5. [θ] as in *think* _____ _____ for [θ] _____
6. [ð] as in *them* _____ _____ for [ð] _____
7. [ʃ] as in *shoe* _____ _____ for [ʃ] _____
8. [tʃ] as in *chair* _____ _____ for [tʃ] _____
9. [ʒ] as in *rouge* _____ _____ for [ʒ] _____
10. [dʒ] as in *jaw* _____ _____ for [dʒ] _____
11. [j] as in *you* _____ _____ for [j] _____
12. [p] as in *pay* _____ _____ for [p] _____
13. [b] as in *boy* _____ _____ for [b] _____
14. [f] as in *foot* _____ _____ for [f] _____
15. [v] as in *very* _____ _____ for [v] _____
16. [k] as in *key* _____ _____ for [k] _____
17. [g] as in *go* _____ _____ for [g] _____
18. [w] as in *we* _____ _____ for [w] _____
19. [r] as in *red* _____ _____ for [r] _____
20. [l] as in *look* _____ _____ for [l] _____

21. [h] as in *hat* _____ _____ _____ for [h]
22. [m] as in *me* _____ _____ _____ for [m]
23. [n] as in *no* _____ _____ _____ for [n]
24. [ŋ] as in *ring* _____ _____ _____ for [ŋ]

Correct **Incorrect** **Comments**

Past Tense

a. [t] as in *washed* _____ _____ _____
b. [d] as in *cleaned* _____ _____ _____
c. [ɪd] as in *rested* _____ _____ _____

Plurals

a. [z] as in *shoes* _____ _____ _____
b. [s] as in *boots* _____ _____ _____
c. [ɪz] as in *dresses* _____ _____ _____

Are final consonants clear? _____

Other Observations:

184 TO THE TEACHER

USING THE MANUAL FOR CLASSROOM INSTRUCTION

Whether you are an instructor of ESL, speech, or accent reduction or a speech pathologist, you will find **English Pronunciation for Spanish Speakers** completely adaptable for classroom or clinical use. The exercises and self-tests in the manual have been tested in the classroom and have proven to be effective with nonnative speakers of English striving to improve their American English pronunciation. The manual is so complete that it eliminates the need for you to spend endless hours preparing drill materials. The following are some suggestions to help you use the manual effectively.

To the Student

Read this section first to familiarize yourself with the organization and content of the manual.

Sequence of Material

The order of sound presentation is flexible. The integrity of the program will remain intact if you assign the chapters in a sequence of your own choosing. Your personal teaching philosophy, available time, and students' specific needs should dictate what you teach first. Many students will not have difficulty with all the sounds. Consequently, you may wish to skip some chapters completely and spend more time on the **real trouble makers** (like [ʤ] as in *jaw* or [j] as in *you*)!

A Key to Pronouncing the Consonants of American English

In this section you are introduced to the International Phonetic Alphabet. Don't be concerned if you are currently unfamiliar with the phonetic symbols. Each symbol is introduced and explained one at a time. You will learn them easily and gradually as you progress through the program with your students. Refer back to the **Key to Pronouncing the Consonants of American English** (p. 8) when you need to refresh your memory. You may also wish to refer to the **Consonant Review Chart** on page 187 for a quick reference.

Adaptation of Material

The material presented in each chapter can be adapted easily. If your students require more drill at the sentence level before progressing to dialogues or paragraphs, focus your attention on the appropriate exercises; defer presentation of more difficult activities to a later time.

Self-Tests

The self-tests can be used in a variety of ways: (1) You can present the tests as described in the manual to evaluate your students' progress. (2) You can use them as both **PRE** and **POST** tests to measure their gains more precisely. (3) You might prefer to divide your students into "teams" to complete the tests as a group rather than individually. (4) You can assign the self-tests as "homework" to encourage out-of-class practice.

For an Encore

The activities in this section can easily be expanded for classroom use. The diversity of these assignments will certainly liven up the regular classroom routine. For example, in Chapter 1 the students are asked to read several advertisements in the local paper and identify phrases pronounced with the target sounds. This activity could be expanded in the classroom by having students read their ads aloud to each other.

SUPPLEMENTARY ACTIVITIES

As an extra bonus, here are some additional in-class activities to vary your presentation of the material in the manual.

CONSONANT REVIEW CHART

Place of Articulation	Type of Sound						
	Stops		Nasals	Continuants		Affricates	
	voiceless	voiced	voiced	voiceless	voiced	voiceless	voiced
Both lips	/p/	/b/	/m/		/w/		
Upper teeth touch bottom lip				/f/	/v/		
Tongue tip between teeth				/θ/	/ð/		
Tongue tip touches or is near gum ridge	/t/	/d/	/n/	/s/	/z/j/l/		
Tongue touches or is near gum ridge and hard palate				/ʃ/	/ʒ/r/	/tʃ/	/dʒ/
Back of tongue touches soft palate	/k/	/g/	/ŋ/				
Level of vocal cords				/h/			

Objective: To increase the students' ability to recognize the target consonant auditorily.

    Activity 1: Read Exercise A words orally in mixed order. Have the students identify the target consonant as occurring in either the initial, medial, or final position.

    Activity 2: Read phrase and sentence exercises orally. Have the students list all the words containing the target consonant.

Objective: To increase the students' ability to discriminate between the target consonant and their error.

    Activity 1: Use minimal pairs exercises/self-tests (e.g., Exercise B on page 33). Create word pairs such as **thank–sank** and **sank–sank**. Have the students identify the words in each pair as being the SAME or DIFFERENT.

    Activity 2: Read orally from the minimal pairs exercises. Vary the order of the words (**thank–sank sick–thick**). Have the students indicate whether they heard the target vowel in the first or second word.

    Activity 3: Give a "spelling test." Read individual words from the minimal pairs exercises. Have your students write the words as you say them. This is a sure way to determine if they are hearing the target sound.

    Activity 4: Read the phrase and sentence exercises orally. Alternate between imitating a student's typical error and pronouncing the target sound correctly. Have your students determine whether or not the words in the phrases and sentences have been produced accurately.

Objective: To increase the students' ability to produce the target consonant.

    Activity 1: Have your students role-play, using the self-test dialogues at the end of each chapter.

    Activity 2: Play a memory game using the word lists in the manual. Ask one student to complete a sentence with a word containing the target consonant. The next student must repeat the sentence and add another word with the target sound.

Example for target consonant [v]: "I'm going on **vacation** and **I've** packed a **vest, vase, stove** . . . ."

Objective: To increase the students' ability to correctly pronounce past tense and plural endings.

Activity 1: Play a question and answer game using regular present and past tense verbs. Ask one student to respond in a complete sentence to your question; then ask a yes or no question of another student. The next student must respond to the question, pronouncing the verb correctly in the past tense, and ask a question of his own. (Example: *"When did you stop smoking?"* *"I stopped smoking last year!"* *"Did you shine your car today? "No, I shined it yesterday."*)

Activity 2: Present a variety of three-verb series aloud. (One past tense verb in each series should have a different *ed* sound than the other two.) Ask the students to identify the verb with the different *ed* sound. (Example: You say *baked, cleaned, cooked*; the students should select *cleaned*.)

Activity 3: Play a "bragging" game using various noun categories. (Example: One student says, *"I have two **cars**! How many **cars** do you have?"* "I
       [z]   [z]

have three **cars**! and two **boats**"; or "I ate four
       [z]   [s]

eggs and two **pieces** of bacon. What did you
 [z]   [ɪz]

eat?" etc.).

With all these suggestions and the activities described in the manual, your students will be kept occupied and learning throughout the course!

```
*********************************
```

APPENDIX

```
*********************************
```

ANSWERS TO SELF-TEST I ON PAGES 13–14.

1. school   Ⓒ   I   6. study   Ⓒ   I

2. estart   C   Ⓘ   7. eslow   C   Ⓘ

3. estudent   C   Ⓘ   8. skating   Ⓒ   I

4. snake   Ⓒ   I   9. esalad   C   Ⓘ

5. esmoking   C   Ⓘ   10. stealing   Ⓒ   I

ANSWERS TO SELF-TEST I ON PAGE 17.

1. s u p p o Ⓢ e   6. s a l e Ⓢ m a n

2. S u Ⓢ a n   7. s e a Ⓢ o n

3. d i Ⓢ a s t e r   8. r e Ⓢ i s t

4. e a Ⓢ i e s t   9. p r e Ⓢ e n t s

5. t i s s u e Ⓢ   10. b u Ⓢ i n e s s

ANSWERS TO SELF-TEST II ON PAGE 17.

1. eyes   nose   (wrist)   ears

2. walls   (waltz)   wells   ways

3. (carrots)   apples   peas   raisins

4. pleasing   pleasant   (pleasure)   please

5. deserve   daisy   (serve)   design

6. (cease)   seize   size   sings

7. Tuesday   Thursday   Wednesday   (Saturday)

8. (east)   ease   easy   tease

9. rose   (rice)   raise   rise

10. (fox)   xylophone   clothes   zero

ANSWERS TO SELF-TEST I ON PAGE 20.

1. 1 2 ③   (peace   peace   peas)
2. 1 ② 3   (rise   rice   rise)
3. ① 2 3   (raise   race   race)
4. 1 ② 3   (Sue   zoo   Sue)
5. 1 2 ③   (racer   racer   razor)

6.   1 2 ③   (lose   lose   loose)
7.   ① 2 3   (plays   place   place)
8.   ① 2 3   (phase   face   face)
9.   1 ② 3   (zeal   seal   zeal)
10. 1 2 ③   (eyes   eyes   ice)

ANSWERS TO SELF-TEST II ON PAGE 20.

    [s]   [s]   [z]
1. **It's** raining **cats** and **dogs**. (*Llueve a cántaros.*)

    [z] [s] [z]   [s]
2. Come **as soon as possible**.

    [s]   [z]
3. **Strike** while the iron **is** hot. (*Aprovecharse de la ocasión.*)

       [z]   [s]
4. Kill two **birds** with one **stone**. (*Matar dos pájaros de un tiro.*)

    [z]   [z]
5. **Misery loves** company. (*Mal de muchos consuelo de todos.*)

ANSWERS TO SELF-TEST III ON PAGE 21.

1. We finally won the   ⟮(race⟯   raise).
                    [s]   [z]

2. I know that   ⟮(face⟯   phase).
             [s]   [z]

3. He gave me a good   (price   ⟮prize⟯).
                   [s]   [z]

4. Look at her small   ⟮(niece⟯   knees).
                  [s]   [z]

5. We must accept the   ⟮(loss⟯   laws).
                   [s]   [z]

6. The sheep have   (fleece   ⟮fleas⟯).
               [s]   [z]

7. Did you hear the   (bus   ⟮buzz⟯)?
                 [s]   [z]

8. His dog has a large   (muscle   ⟮muzzle⟯).
                   [s]   [z]

9. How much is the (sink) zinc)?
   [s] [z]

10. I can identify the (spice spies)
    [s] [z]

ANSWERS TO SELF-TEST IV ON PAGE 22.

A Man Named (Stu)

A man from (Texas) named (Stu)

Was crazy about (Silly) (Sue.)

   He proposed twenty times,

   Using (song,) (dance,) and rhymes

Until (Sue) (said) to (Stu,) "I do!"

A Girl Named (Maxine)

There was a (slim) girl called (Maxine)

She loved cooking (Spanish) cuisine

   She (spent) days eating (rice,)

   (Lots) of chickens and (spice)

Now (Maxine) is no longer lean!

ANSWERS TO SELF-TEST I ON PAGE 26.

1. (t)raction
2. tha(t)
3. patien(t)
4. (t)exture
5. (t)emperature
6. (t)ooth
7. presen(t)ation
8. arithme(t)ic
9. (t)ogether
10. sub(t)raction

ANSWERS TO SELF-TEST II ON PAGE 26.

1. (two (too)) **Tess** had _____ much **to eat**.

2. ((two) too) I **must return** _____ books.

3. ((right) write) "**Two** wrongs **don't** make a _____."

4. (right (write)) Please _____ me a **note**.

5. ((aunt) ant) **Tim's** _____ is **twenty-two**.

ANSWERS TO SELF-TEST III ON PAGE 26.

TOM: (Teresa,) who were you (talking) (to) on the (telephone?)

TERESA: (Terry) (White.) She (wanted) to know (what) (time) the (party) is (tonight.)

TOM: (Terry) is always (late.) She missed* the (tennis) (tournament) (last) (Tuesday.)

TERESA: (Two) days ago, she came (to) (breakfast) (at) (two) instead of (ten) A.M.

TOM: (Terry) (missed) her (flight) (to) (Texas) (last) week.

TERESA: She's never on (time) for any (appointment.)

TOM: This is (terrible!) (What) (time) did you (tell) her (to) come (tonight?)

TERESA: (Don't) worry. I had a (terrific) idea. I (told) (Terry) (to) come (at) six (fifteen.) The (party) really is (set) for (eight!)

TOM: (To) (tell) the (truth,) I wish you (told) her it was (at) (two) (fifteen.) I just (don't) (trust) her!

ANSWERS TO SELF-TEST I ON PAGE 30.

1. (C) I (The **bride** is very lovely.)

2. C (I) (The **bat** children were punished.)

3. C (I) (Be careful when you climb the **lather**.)

4. (C) I (Mother was **mad** at us.)

5. C (I) (Plant the **seat** and a flower will grow.)

*The letters -ed in 'missed" sound like [t]. (Refer to p. 159, Pronouncing Past Tense Verbs.)

ANSWERS TO SELF-TEST II ON PAGE 31.

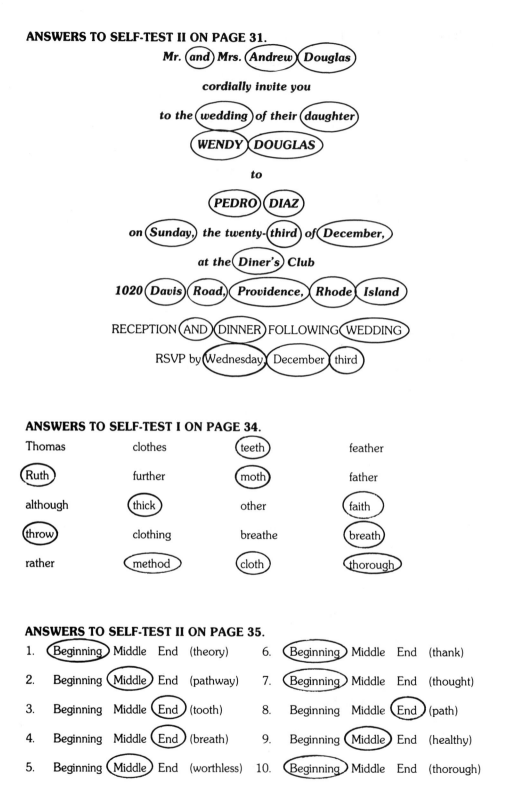

Mr. (and) Mrs. (Andrew)(Douglas)

cordially invite you

to the (wedding) of their (daughter)

(WENDY)(DOUGLAS)

to

(PEDRO)(DIAZ)

on (Sunday,) the twenty-(third) of (December,)

at the (Diner's) Club

1020 (Davis)(Road,)(Providence,)(Rhode)(Island)

RECEPTION (AND)(DINNER) FOLLOWING (WEDDING)

RSVP by (Wednesday,)(December)(third)

ANSWERS TO SELF-TEST I ON PAGE 34.

Thomas	clothes	(teeth)	feather
(Ruth)	further	(moth)	father
although	(thick)	other	(faith)
(throw)	clothing	breathe	(breath)
rather	(method)	(cloth)	(thorough)

ANSWERS TO SELF-TEST II ON PAGE 35.

1. (Beginning) Middle End (theory)
2. Beginning (Middle) End (pathway)
3. Beginning Middle (End) (tooth)
4. Beginning Middle (End) (breath)
5. Beginning (Middle) End (worthless)
6. (Beginning) Middle End (thank)
7. (Beginning) Middle End (thought)
8. Beginning Middle (End) (path)
9. Beginning (Middle) End (healthy)
10. (Beginning) Middle End (thorough)

ANSWERS TO SELF-TEST III ON PAGE 35.

Do you know (anything) about Jim (Thorpe?) He was an American Indian (athlete.) He excelled in (everything) at the Olympics. (Thousands) were angry when (Thorpe's) medals were taken away because he was called a professional (athlete.) In 1973, long after his (death,) (Thorpe's) medals were restored. (Throughout) the world, Jim (Thorpe) is (thought) to be one of the greatest male (athletes.)

ANSWERS TO SELF-TEST I ON PAGE 40.

1. B (M) E (clothing)	6. B M (E) (breathe)
2. B M (E) (loathe)	7. B (M) E (gathering)
3. (B) M E (these)	8. (B) M E (though)
4. B (M) E (northern)	9. (B) M E (therefore)
5. B (M) E (smoother)	10. B M (E) (soothe)

ANSWERS TO SELF-TEST II ON PAGE 40.

1. (This (These)) _____ shoes are **weatherproof.**

2. ((weather) whether) I **loathe** this wet _____.

3. ((This) These) _____ board is **smoother than the other** one.

4. ((there) their) **The** family will be _____ for **the** wedding.

5. (they (them)) **Mother** told _____ not to be late.

6. ((They) Them) _____ are **worthy** of **the** award.

7. ((Those) That) _____ **brothers** are **rather** tall.

8. (weather (whether)) I don't know _____ to buy **this** one or **that** one.

9. ((That) Those) _____ **lather** is **soothing.**

10. ((Their) There) _____ **father** likes **the weather** in **southern** Florida.

ANSWERS TO SELF-TEST III ON PAGE 41.

(The) *Photo Album*

DAUGHTER: (Mother,) I would like (these) old pictures. Who's (this?)

MOTHER: (That's) your great (grandmother.)

DAUGHTER: (The) (feathered) hat is funny! Who's (that) man?

MOTHER: (That's) your (grandfather.) He was from (the) (Netherlands.)

DAUGHTER: I know (these) people! Aren't (they) Uncle Tom and Uncle Bob?

MOTHER: (That's) right. (Those) are my (brothers.) (They) always (bothered) me!

DAUGHTER: (This) must be (either) (father) or his (brother.)

MOTHER: (Neither!) (That's) your (father's) uncle.

DAUGHTER: Why are (there) (other) people in (this) photo?

MOTHER: (This) was a family (gathering.) We got (together) all the time.

DAUGHTER: (Mother,) who's (this) ("smooth") -looking man?

MOTHER: Shhhhhhhhh! I'd (rather) not say. Your (father) will hear!

DAUGHTER: Is (that) your old boyfriend?

MOTHER: Well, even (mothers) had fun in (those) days!

ANSWERS TO REVIEW TEST I ON PAGE 44.

　　5　2
1. thousand

　　1　5　1
2. southwest

　　6　2
3. these

　　　5　3
4. athlete

　　　5　　　4
5. birthday card

196 APPENDIX

ANSWERS TO REVIEW TEST II ON PAGE 44.

1.	5	[θ]	think	through	thought	another
2.	2	[z]	rice	rise	raisin	phase
3.	4	[d]	duck	soldier	deep	fed
4.	6	[ð]	weather	cloth	their	bathe
5.	3	[t]	Tim	Terry	Thomas	Beth

ANSWERS TO REVIEW TEST III ON PAGE 45.

1. Did you make the ((bed) bet)?
   [d]   [t]

2. The doctors didn't use (either (ether)).
   [ð]   [θ]

3. Steven doesn't like to miss ((math) Mass).
   [ð]   [s]

4. It is a ((worthy) wordy) article.
   [ð]   [d]

5. I like to ((raise) race) horses.
   [z]   [v]

6. Please give him the (time (dime)).
   [t]   [d]

7. They announced the ((truth) truce).
   [θ]   [s]

8. (Teasing (teething)) makes the baby cry.
   [z]   [ð]

9. The boy doesn't want to ((think) sink).
   [θ]   [s]

10. Before you know it, (they (day)) will be here.
    [ð]   [d]

ANSWERS TO REVIEW TEST IV ON PAGE 46.

<u>3</u> <u>1</u> <u>1</u>
Let Us Smile

<u>6</u> <u>5</u> <u>6</u> <u>2</u>   <u>6</u>
The thing that goes the farthest,

<u>3</u>   <u>2</u>   <u>5</u>
towards making life worthwhile,

<u>6</u>   <u>1</u>   <u>3</u> <u>4</u> <u>2</u>   <u>3</u>
That costs the least, and does the most,

<u>2</u>   <u>2</u> <u>3</u><u>1</u>
is just a pleasant smile!

<u>1</u>   <u>5</u>   <u>4</u> <u>1</u>
It's full of worth and goodness too,

<u>6</u>   <u>4</u>   <u>3</u>
with manly kindness blent,

<u>5</u>   <u>4</u> <u>2</u>
It's worth a million dollars,

<u>4</u> <u>2</u>   <u>1</u>
and it doesn't cost a cent!

ANSWERS TO SELF-TEST I ON PAGE 49.

1.	crush	cash	(catch)	crash
2.	chef	(chief)	chute	chiffon
3.	machine	parachute	mustache	(kitchen)
4.	(China)	Russia	Chicago	Michigan
5.	musician	physician	(chemist)	electrician
6.	pressure	(pressed)	assure	permission
7.	(division)	subtraction	addition	multiplication
8.	position	action	(patio)	motion
9.	Charlotte	Cheryl	Sharon	(Charles)
10.	tension	(resign)	pension	mention

ANSWERS TO SELF-TEST I ON PAGE 53.

1. C (I) (That store has **sheep** prices.)

2. (C) I (I ate **chicken** and rice for dinner.)

3. C (I) (My **wash** tells perfect time.)

4. C (I) (He couldn't **cash** the ball.)

5. C (I) (I bought new **choose**.)

6. (C) I (We met the first-grade **teacher**.)

7. (C) I (**March** is a windy month.)

8. (C) I (Can you **reach** the top shelf?)

9. C (I) (Please light the **mash**.)

10. (C) I (How many **children** do you have?)

ANSWERS TO SELF-TEST I ON PAGE 55.

1. 1 (2) 3 (share chair share)   6. 1 2 (3) (she's she's cheese)

2. 1 2 (3) (chop chop shop)   7. 1 (2) 3 (chin shin chin)

3. 1 2 (3) (mush mush much)   8. 1 2 (3) (sheep sheep cheap)

4. 1 2 (3) (cash cash catch)   9. (1) 2 3 (chew shoe shoe)

5. 1 2 (3) (witch witch wish)   10. (1) 2 3 (dish ditch ditch)

ANSWERS TO SELF-TEST II ON PAGE 55.

    [ʃ]   [tʃ]   [ʃ]
1. The puppy **shouldn't chew** the **shoes**.

  [ʃ]   [tʃ]   [ʃ]
2. **Shine** the **furniture** with **polish**.

   [ʃ]   [ʃ] [ʃ]
3. The **chef** prepared a **special dish**.

  [ʃ]   [tʃ]   [ʃ]
4. We **should change** the dirty **sheets**.

 [tʃ]   [ʃ]   [tʃ]
5. **Choosing** a **profession** is a **challenge**.

ANSWERS TO SELF-TEST III ON PAGE 56.

1. I didn't see the (dish) ditch).
                 [ʃ]   [tʃ]

2. He hurt his (shin (chin).
             [ʃ]   [tʃ]

3. Did you hear that (shatter) chatter)?
               [ʃ]   [tʃ]

4. It's a silly (wish) witch).
             [ʃ]   [tʃ]

5. It was an endless (marsh (march)).
   [ʃ]   [tʃ]

6. She brought me the (wash watch).
   [ʃ]   [tʃ]

7. They have a large (share (chair)).
   [ʃ]   [tʃ]

8. We must fix the (ship chip).
   [ʃ]   [tʃ]

9. Does she have a new (crush (crutch))?
   [ʃ]   [tʃ]

10. They completed the (shore (chore)).
    [ʃ]   [tʃ]

ANSWERS TO SELF-TEST IV ON PAGE 57.

CHAVO: Hi, (Marshall.) Do you have any change for the (washing) (machine?)

MARSHALL: Chavo, what are you doing (washing) clothes?

CHAVO: My wife, (Sharon,) is visiting family in (Michigan.) I'm watching the children.

MARSHALL: Watch out! Don't put bleach on those (shirts.) You'll (wash) out the color.

CHAVO: Will you teach me how to (wash) clothes?

MARSHALL: Be (sure) to (wash) white (shirts) separately. Don't use too much soap.

CHAVO: I (wish) (Sharon) would return. It's more natural for a woman to (wash) and (shop.)

MARSHALL: You sound like a (chauvinist!) I don't mind doing chores. I'm great in the kitchen, too!

CHAVO: Would you like to take charge? I'll cheerfully pay you (cash!)

MARSHALL: Listen old chap—I'm a bachelor and too old to chase after children. I'm in a (rush.) It's been nice chatting with you, Chavo.

CHAVO: (Sure)—nice chatting with you too, (Marshall.)

ANSWERS TO SELF-TEST I ON PAGE 60.

1. leisure   pleasure   (sure)   measure

2. Asia   Asian   Parisian   (Paris)

3. (huge)   beige   rouge   prestige

4. (passion)   collision   occasion   decision

5. massage   mirage   (message)   corsage

6. confusion   (conclusive) contusion   conclusion

200 APPENDIX

7. lesion (profession) explosion aversion

8. vision version television (visible)

9. seizure (seize) azure division

10. treasury treasurer (treason) treasure

ANSWERS TO SELF-TEST II ON PAGE 61.

      [ʃ]   [ʒ]
1. The **commission** made a **decision**.

              [ʒ]   [ʃ]
2. The class learned **division** and **addition**.

   [ʒ]   [ʒ]
3. **Measure** the **garage**.

      [ʃ]   [ʒ]
4. Your **profession** has **prestige**.

      [ʒ] [ʃ]   [ʒ]
5. That's an **unusual shade** of **rouge**.

ANSWERS TO SELF-TEST III ON PAGE 61.

Good evening. This is (Frazier) White with the 10:00 P.M. (television) news. Here are some (unusual) items.

**** Tourists on a (pleasure) trip discovered buried (treasure.) The (treasure) dates back to ancient (Persia.)

**** An (explosion) took place in a (garage) on First Avenue. (Seizure) of a bomb was made after much (confusion.)

****(Asian) flu is spreading. (Asian) flu vaccinations will be available to those with (exposure) to the germ.

**** Today was the (Parisian) fashion show. Everything from (casual) (leisure) clothes to (negligees) was shown. (Beige) is the big color. Hemlines (measure) two inches below the knee.

In (conclusion,) carry your raincoat. (Occasional) showers are due tomorrow. Hope your evening is a (pleasure.) This is (Frazier) White saying GOOD NIGHT!

ANSWERS TO SELF-TEST I ON PAGE 66.

(Java)   Guatemala   (Jerusalem)   Greece

England   (Germany)   (Jamaica)   Hungary

(Japan)   Greenland   (Algeria)   (Egypt)

(Belgium)   (Argentina)   China   Luxembourg

ANSWERS TO SELF-TEST II ON PAGE 66.

1. bulge   (bug)   budge   badge

2. major   soldier   general   (captain)

3. gentle   gem   intelligent   (hen)

4. angel   (angle)   age   adjective

5. jug   July   (hug)   juice

6. giant   gin   (gill)   giraffe

7. educate   graduate   cordial   (duck)

8. (lung)   lunge   lounge   large

9. Jill   Gene   Joan   (Gary)

10. Germany   (Greenland)   Georgia   Virginia

ANSWERS TO SELF-TEST I ON PAGE 70.

1. The **youth** left. He hasn't come back **YET**.

2. The player ran 50 **yards**. The crowds began to **YELL**.

3. Today is Monday. **YESTERDAY** was Sunday.

4. Egg **yolks** should be **YELLOW**.

5. **You** should get a check-up once a **YEAR**.

ANSWERS TO SELF-TEST II ON PAGE 70.

1. (SAME) DIFFERENT   (I had to **yawn**. I had to **yawn**.)

2. SAME (DIFFERENT)   (Did you say **yacht**? Did you say **jot**?)

3. SAME (DIFFERENT)   (It's not **yellow**. It's not **Jello**.)

4. (SAME) DIFFERENT   (They left **yesterday**. They left **yesterday**.)

5. SAME (DIFFERENT)   (Find the **major**. Find the **mayor**.)

ANSWERS TO SELF-TEST I ON PAGE 72.

1. jet (yet)

2. (joke) yolk

3. jot (yacht)

4. Jew (you)

5. (juice) use

ANSWERS TO SELF-TEST II ON PAGE 72.

1. Yale _____ (*Jail* is a famous university.)
2. yam _____ (A *jam* is like a sweet potato.)
3. yellow _____ (*Jello* is my favorite color.)
4. yolk _____ (An egg *joke* is yellow.)
5. year _____ (What *jeer* were you born?)
6. juice _____ (Do you like orange *use*?)
7. jet _____ (A 747 is a large *yet*.)
8. yacht _____ (We took a cruise on a *jot*.)
9. jewel _____ (A ruby is a precious *you'll*.)
10. jokes _____ (People play *yokes* on April Fools Day.)

ANSWERS TO SELF-TEST III ON PAGE 73.

Do you know what YANKEE means? People from the United States are (generally) called Yankees. (Soldiers) from the northern (region) were called Yankees during the Civil War. (George) M. Cohan wrote a (stage) hit called Yankee Doodle Dandy. (Jealous) baseball fans (waged) war over the New York Yankees and (Dodgers) for years. Whether you are from (Georgia) or New (Jersey,) you should (enjoy) being called a Yank!

ANSWERS TO REVIEW TEST I ON PAGE 76.

	2	3	1			3	2	1
1.	cheer	jeer	year	6.	chin	shin	gin
	3	2	1			2	3	1
2.	cheap	jeep	sheep	7.	choke	joke	yolk
	1	3	2			1	3	2
3.	chew	shoe	you	8.	cherry	Jerry	Sherry
	1	2	3			2	1	3
4.	cello	Jello	yellow	9.	your	chore	shore
	2	1	3			2	1	3
5.	choose	shoes	Jews	10.	chose	shows	Joe's

ANSWERS TO REVIEW TEST II ON PAGE 77.

1. __5__ [j]
onion
union
million
billion

2. __1__ [ʃ]
chef
chute
chic
chiffon

3. __2__ [tʃ]
nature
picture
capture
furniture

4. __3__ [ʒ]
division
occasion
explosion
television

5. __1__ [ʃ]
Russia
tissue
passion
mission

6. __4__ [ʤ]
gradual
cordial
soldier
education

7. __2__ [tʃ]
chief
catch
question
ketchup

8. __5__ [j]
cute
yawn
amuse
senior

9. __4__ [ʤ]
ridge
angel
suggest
general

10. __3__ [ʒ]
vision
rouge
garage
pleasure

ANSWERS TO REVIEW TEST III ON PAGE 78.

1. The (sheep jeep) is very old.
　　　[ʃ]　　[ʤ]

2. The (legion lesion) is large.
　　　[ʤ]　　[ʒ]

3. My friend (Sherry Jerry) is nice.
　　　　　[ʃ]　　[ʤ]

4. The (cash catch) was counted.
　　　[ʃ]　　[tʃ]

5. I don't like (Jello yellow).
　　　　　　[ʤ]　　[j]

6. The (mayor major) made a speech.
　　　[j]　　[ʤ]

7. The crowd (cheered jeered) loudly.
　　　　　　[tʃ]　　[ʤ]

8. The (dishes ditches) are dirty.
　　　[ʃ]　　[tʃ]

204 APPENDIX

9. The (badge [dʒ] / batch [tʃ]) was given out.

10. Did you see the (etching [tʃ] / edging [dʒ])?

ANSWERS TO REVIEW TEST IV ON PAGE 79.

1. [tʃ] [ʃ] **([dʒ])** (Joan   Jerry   George)
2. **([tʃ])** [ʃ] [dʒ] (cheese chart   chick)
3. **([tʃ])** [ʃ] [dʒ] (catch   match   teach)
4. [tʃ] **([ʃ])** [dʒ] (show   she's   share)
5. **([dʒ])** [j] [tʃ] (engine major pajamas)
6. **([dʒ])** [j] [tʃ] (bridge   judge   age)
7. [dʒ] **([j])** [tʃ] (yes   young   you)
8. **([ʃ])** [ʒ] [dʒ] (rush   wash   wish)
9. [ʃ] **([ʒ])** [dʒ] (measure usual   beige)
10. **([ʃ])** [ʒ] [dʒ] (shelf   Chicago shock)

ANSWERS TO REVIEW TEST VI ON PAGE 80.

[ʃ] as in *shoe*	[tʃ] as in *chair*	[ʒ] as in *beige*	[dʒ] as in *jam*	[j] as in *you*
Washington	much	measured	George	united
contributions	chopped	unusual	just	year
shows	cherry	decisions	courage	contributions
revolution	charge		Virginia	unusual
showed	chief		legend	future
compassion	future		general	
constitutional			soldiers	
convention			forge	
nation			charge	
generations			generations	
shall				

ANSWERS TO SELF-TEST I ON PAGE 83.

1. A nickname for **Peter** is Pete _____.
2. The **opposite** of war is peace _____.
3. **Pam** bought peanuts _____ to feed the elephants.
4. The **top** of a mountain is called a peak _____.
5. The **plural** of **person** is people _____.
6. A **popular** fruit is a peach _____.
7. A bird with bright feathers is a peacock _____.
8. **Potatoes** should be peeled _____ before being cooked.
9. The letter **preceding** Q is P _____.
10. Something that annoys you is called a "pet peeve _____."

ANSWERS TO SELF-TEST II ON PAGE 83.

The (Surprise) (Trip)

PABLO: (Paulette,) I have a (surprise!) We're taking a (trip) to (Puerto) Rico tonight!

PAULETTE: I'm very (happy.) But I need more time to (prepare.)

PABLO: That's (simple.) I'll (help) you (pack.)

PAULETTE: Who will care for our (pet) (poodle?)

PABLO: Your (parents!)

PAULETTE: Who will (pick) (up) the mail?

PABLO: Our neighbor (Pete!)

PAULETTE: Who will water the (plants?)

PABLO: We'll (put) them on the (patio.)

PAULETTE: Who will (pay) for the (trip?)

PABLO: The (company) is (paying) every (penny!)

PAULETTE: (Pablo,) you've really (planned) this.

PABLO: Of course! I'm (dependable,) (superior,) and a (perfect). . .

PAULETTE: (Pain) in the neck!" Don't get carried away!

ANSWERS TO SELF-TEST I ON PAGE 87.

1. ((bread) bred) I like rye _____.

2. (bear (bare)) Don't walk in your _____ feet.

3. ((been) bin) **Bob** has _____ here **before**.

4. (been (bin)) Please store the **beans** in the _____.

5. ((blew) blue) The wind _____ my **bag** away.

6. (blew (blue)) **Betty's** _____ **bonnet** is **becoming**.

7. ((Buy) By) _____ a **box** of **black buttons**.

8. (berry (bury)) The dog will _____ his **bone** in the **backyard**.

9. ((bored) board) My **brother** drinks **beer** when he's _____.

10. (bored (board)) The **builder** needs a **bigger** _____.

ANSWERS TO SELF-TEST II ON PAGE 88.

BETTY: (Benito,) I (bet) you forgot my (birthday!)

BENITO: I (bet) I didn't. I (bought) you a (birthday) present.

BETTY: I can't (believe) it. What did you (bring?)

206 APPENDIX

BENITO: It begins with the letter B.

BETTY: Oh, boy! It must be a bathrobe. You buy me one every birthday.

BENITO: It's not a bathrobe!

BETTY: Is it a bowling ball?

BENITO: No, it's not a bowling ball.

BETTY: It must be a book about boating, your favorite hobby.

BENITO: Betty, you're way off base. I bought you a bracelet. A diamond bracelet!

BETTY: Wow! This is the best birthday present I ever got. You didn't rob a bank, did you?

BENITO: Don't worry. I didn't beg, borrow, or steal; just don't expect any more presents for a long time. I'm broke!

ANSWERS TO SELF-TEST I ON PAGE 91.

1. **Find** another name **for** a drugstore. pharmacy
2. **Find** another name **for** a doctor. physician
3. **Find** another name **for** a snapshot. photograph
4. **Find** the name **for** a person who studies **philosophy**. philosopher
5. **Find** the short **form** of the word **telephone**. phone
6. **Find** another name **for** a record player. phonograph
7. **Find** the name **for** a person who predicts the **future**. prophet
8. **Find** the name **for** the study of sounds. phonetics
9. **Find** the term that **refers** to your sister's son. nephew
10. **Find** the name **for** a chart showing **figures**. graph

ANSWERS TO SELF-TEST II ON PAGE 92.

Florida was founded by Ponce de Leon in 1513. This famous explorer from Spain was searching for a fountain of youth. He named the land Florida, which means "full of flowers" in Spanish. He failed in his efforts to find the fountain. He finally died after fighting the Indians. Unfortunately, no one has ever found the fountain in Florida or the formula for eternal youth. However, the fun and sun in Florida are enough to attract folks from every hemisphere to this famous American state.

ANSWERS TO SELF-TEST I ON PAGE 95.

1. B M (E) (have)
2. B (M) E (heavy)
3. B (M) E (over)
4. (B) M E (victory)
5. B (M) E (oven)
6. B (M) E (several)
7. B (M) E (clever)
8. B M (E) (love)
9. (B) M E (very)
10. B (M) E (television)

ANSWERS TO SELF-TEST II ON PAGE 96.

1. ((clever) clover cover) **Van** is a _____ student.

2. (clever clover (cover)) I bought a **velvet** _____

3. (berry (very) ferry) **Vera** is _____ pretty.

4. (leaf (leave) live) The train will _____ at **seven**.

5. (leaves (loves) lives) **Vicky** _____ her sons, **Victor** and **Vance**.

ANSWERS TO SELF-TEST III ON PAGE 96.

1. (1) 2 3 (vat fat bat)

2. 1 (2) 3 (beer veer fear)

3. (1) 2 3 (very berry ferry)

4. 1 (2) 3 (robe rove rope)

5. 1 2 (3) (safe sane save)

ANSWERS TO SELF-TEST IV ON PAGE 97.

I (Never) Saw a Moor

I (never) saw a moor,
I (never) saw the sea;
Yet know I how the heather looks,
And what a (wave) must be.

I (never) spoke with God,
Nor (visited) in (Heaven;)
Yet certain am I (of) the spot
As if the chart were (given.)

ANSWERS TO REVIEW TEST I ON PAGE 100.

1. Vera took a   ((bow) vow).
                   [b]   [v]

2. That's a nice   (beach (peach).
                   [b]   [p])

3. There were a lot of ((boats) votes).
                    [b]   [v]

4. We could see her (grief [f] / grieve). [v]

5. I want the (vest [v] / best). [b]

6. He got a good (buy [b] / pie). [p]

7. Don't cut the (vine [v] / fine). [f]

8. The baby sat in his (lap [p] / lab). [b]

9. Can you see the (curb [b] / curve)? [v]

10. The player picked a (five [v] / fife). [f]

ANSWERS TO REVIEW TEST II ON PAGE 101.

1. pills   (The doctor gave me **bills** to ease the pain.)
2. five   (One half of ten is **fife**.)
3. pie   (I like to eat apple **buy**.)
4. very   (The fruit is **berry** sweet.)
5. bag   (Carry the groceries in a paper **back**.)
6. vase   (My flowers are in a glass **phase**.)
7. cab   (He waited an hour for a taxi **cap**.)
8. fender   (His car **vendor** is bent.)
9. have   (I **half** an appointment at noon.)
10. leaving   (Bob is **leafing** town for a week.)

ANSWERS TO REVIEW TEST III ON PAGE 102.

[p]	[b]	[f]	[v]
Aesop's	fable	definition	of
people	valuable	fable	valuable
grapes	brief	brief	very
jumping	by	faults	virtues
up	above	fox	above
probably	but	fine	vine
	became	from	gave
	probably	finally	
	fables	furious	
		left	

ANSWERS TO SELF-TEST I ON PAGE 105.

1. course   count   (choose)   chorus
2. can't   can   (cent)   cone
3. Canada   Texas   Kansas   (Massachusetts)
4. key   keep   keen   (kneel)
5. (celery)   corn   carrots   cabbage
6. mix   box   explain   (xylophone)
7. (knee)   back   ankle   cheek
8. (Charles)   Carol   Chris   Michael
9. mechanic   (much)   chrome   Christmas
10. milk   (cider)   coffee   cream

ANSWERS TO SELF-TEST II ON PAGE 106.

The (American) (Cowboy)

(Americans) (created) the name (cowboy) for the men who (cared) for the (cattle.) You might (recall) the (typical) singing (cowboy) in the movies. He was (kind,) (courageous,) and good-(looking.) He always (caught) the (cow,) (colt,) and of (course,) the girl! But the real (cowboy) was a hard (worker) who had many (difficult) tasks. He had to (take) the (cattle) to (market.) These lonely (cattle) drives (took) many (weeks) through rough (country.) The (cowboy) had to (protect) the (cattle) and (keep) them from running off. In (fact) or (fiction,) the (cowboy) will (continue) to be a (likeable) (American) (character.) *Ride 'em* (cowboy!)

ANSWERS TO SELF-TEST I ON PAGE 109.

1. lag   (lack)
2. (bug)   buck
3. (league)   leak
4. (peg)   peck
5. nag   (knack)

ANSWERS TO SELF-TEST II ON PAGE 110.

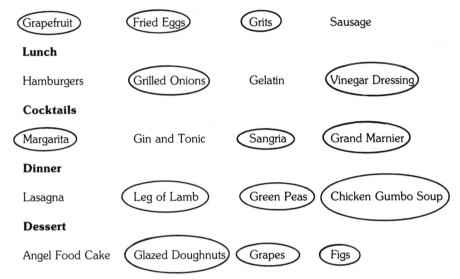

Breakfast

(Grapefruit) (Fried Eggs) (Grits) Sausage

Lunch

Hamburgers (Grilled Onions) Gelatin (Vinegar Dressing)

Cocktails

(Margarita) Gin and Tonic (Sangria) (Grand Marnier)

Dinner

Lasagna (Leg of Lamb) (Green Peas) (Chicken Gumbo Soup)

Dessert

Angel Food Cake (Glazed Doughnuts) (Grapes) (Figs)

ANSWERS TO SELF-TEST I ON PAGE 113.

(week) (someone) (queen) write

(while) who wrong (worry)

whose (waiter) (reward) (square)

guilt (unwilling) saw worthy

(west) lawyer (anywhere) low

ANSWERS TO SELF-TEST II ON PAGE 114.

(Woodrow) (Wilson)

(Woodrow) (Wilson) (was) the (twenty)-fifth president of the United States. He (will) (always) be remembered for his (work) to establish (world) peace. (Wilson) (was) born in 1865 and later (went) to Princeton University. He became president in 1913 and stayed in the (White) House for two terms. His first (wife) died (while) he (was) in office, and he married a (Washington) widow. (When) the United States entered (World) (War) (I) in 1917, (Wilson) quickly provided the needed (wisdom.) After the (war,) (Wilson) made a (nationwide) tour to (win) support for the League of Nations. (Wilson) (was) (awarded) the Nobel Prize for his (worthwhile) (work) for peace. He died in (1924.) (Everywhere) in the (world,) (Wilson) (was) thought of as a (wise) and (wonderful) leader.

ANSWERS TO SELF-TEST III ON PAGE 114.

1. **When** **was** **Woodrow** **Wilson** born?
   Woodrow **Wilson** **was** born in ___1865___.

2. How many **wives** did **Wilson** have **while** in the **White** House?
   Wilson had ___two___ **wives**.

3. **When** did the United States enter **World War I**?
   The United States entered **World War I** in 1917___.

4. **Why** **was** **Wilson** **awarded** the Nobel Prize?
   Wilson **was** **awarded** the Nobel Prize for his worthwhile work for peace.

5. **Where** **was** **Wilson** thought of as a **wise and wonderful** leader?
   Wilson **was** thought of as a **wise and wonderful** leader everywhere in the world.

ANSWERS TO SELF-TEST I ON PAGE 118.

1. If you are **located** in **Dublin**, you **live** in Ireland___.
2. If you are **located** in **London**, you **live** in England___.
3. If you are **located** in **Los Angeles**, you **live** in California___.
4. If you are **located** in **Lisbon**, you **live** in Portugal___.
5. If you are **located** in **Lucerne**, you **live** in Switzerland___.
6. If you are **located** in **Milan**, you **live** in Italy___.
7. If you are **located** in **São Paolo**, you **live** in Brazil___.
8. If you are **located** in **Brussels**, you **live** in Belgium___.
9. If you are **located** in **Orlando**, you **live** in Florida___.
10. If you are **located** in **New Orleans**, you **live** in Louisiana___.

ANSWERS TO SELF-TEST II ON PAGE 119.

LILLIAN: (Allan,) I just had a (telephone) (call) from Aunt (Lola.) (Uncle) (Bill) died.

ALLAN: The (uncle) who was a (millionaire?)

LILLIAN: Yes. He (lived) (alone) in (California.)

ALLAN: Did he (leave) us any money?

LILLIAN: The (lawyer) is reading the (will) at (11:00.) I (really) don't (believe) he (left) his (family) anything!

ALLAN: (Uncle) (Bill) had to (leave) something to a (relative.)

LILLIAN: He (lived) with (lots) of (animals.) He didn't (like) (people.)

ALLAN: (Hold) it! (I'll) answer the (telephone) (*(Allan)* hangs up the phone.) (Well,) (Lillian,) you're out of (luck!) (Uncle) (Bill) (left) (all) his ("loot") to the (Animal) (Lovers') (League.)

LILLIAN: Do you think (Lulu,) our (poodle,) is (eligible) for a (little?)

212 APPENDIX

ANSWERS TO SELF-TEST I ON PAGE 122.

1. This **creature** has black and white **stripes**. This **creature** is a zebra_____.
2. This **forest creature** has long **ears** and is a **celebrity** at **Easter**. This **creature** is a rabbit_____.
3. This **creature** has **large antlers** and is **around** at **Christmas**. This **creature** is a reindeer_____.
4. This **creature** has spots and a **very** long neck. This **creature** is a giraffe_____.
5. This **creature** lives in the **arctic**, is **large**, and is **very hungry**. This **creature** is a **polar bear**_____.
6. This **forest creature carries her** babies in a pouch. This **creature** is a kangaroo_____.
7. This **friendly creature "croaks"** and says **"rivet, rivet."** This **creature** is a frog_____.
8. This **forest creature** is a **very** talkative **bird**. This **colorful creature** is a parrot_____.
9. This **fierce creature** has black and yellow **stripes**. This **ferocious creature** is a tiger_____.
10. This **graceful creature started** as a **caterpillar**. This **pretty creature** is a butterfly_____.

ANSWERS TO SELF-TEST II ON PAGE 123.

(Robin) Hood

The (story) of (Robin) Hood has been (retold) many times. (Robin) Hood was an outlaw who lived in (Sherwood) (Forest.) He lived (there) with Maid (Marian,) (Friar) Tuck, and (others.) (Robin) was (really) a (hero) (rather) than a (criminal.) He (robbed) the (rich) and gave to the (poor.) He was a (remarkable) (marksman) with his bow and (arrow.) The (story) of (Robin) Hood has been (written) about and (dramatized) since the eleventh (century.) (Robin) (truly) (represents) a (righteous) (figure) opposing (cruelty) and (greed.)

ANSWERS TO SELF-TEST I ON PAGE 127.

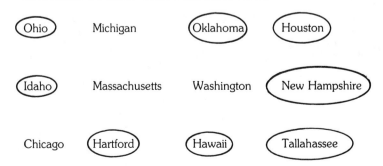

(Ohio)   Michigan   (Oklahoma)   (Houston)

(Idaho)   Massachusetts   Washington   (New Hampshire)

Chicago   (Hartford)   (Hawaii)   (Tallahassee)

ANSWERS TO SELF-TEST II ON PAGE 127.

HELEN: (Hi,) Mom. Welcome (home.) (How) was (Hawaii?)
MOTHER: Like a second (honeymoon!) I'm as (happy) as a lark. (How) are you?
HELEN: (Horrible!) (Henry) is in the (hospital) with a broken (hip.)
MOTHER: (How) did that happen?
HELEN: He (heard) a noise outside. (He) went (behind) the (house) and fell over a (hose.)
MOTHER: (How) are my (handsome) grandsons?
HELEN: They won't (behave.) And my (housekeeper) (had) to quit.
MOTHER: (Perhaps) you'd like me to (help) at (home.)
HELEN: Oh, Mom, I was (hoping) you'd say that. (Hurry) to the (house) as soon as possible.
MOTHER: I guess the (honeymoon) is over. (Here) we go again!

ANSWERS TO REVIEW TEST I ON PAGE 132.

1. Leave it in the (back (bag).
         [k]   [g]

2. I think it's (good (wood).
         [g]   [w]

3. Do you like the (rhyme (lime)?
         [r]   [l]

4. His name is ((Gil) Will).
         [g] [w]

5. She needs a bigger ((lock) log).
         [k] [g]

6. Turn toward the (light (right).
         [l] [r]

7. They really ((ate) hate) the cake.
         [h]

8. My teacher ((collected) corrected) the papers.
         [l]   [r]

9. Give him the ((coat) goat).
         [k] [g]

10. Who asked for ((jelly) Jerry)?
          [l] [r]

ANSWERS TO REVIEW TEST II ON PAGE 133.

[k] as in *cake*	[g] as in *go*	[l] as in *lamp*	[r] as in *red*	[w] as in *we*	[h] as in *hat*
explain	grass	blame	written	square	whole
coast	ghost	simple	pour	awake	whose
queer	regular	listen	there	one	somehow
ticket	league	meal	wrist	we	inhale
chorus	brag	billion	brave	weather	history
fix		salad	write	western	
kitten				wind	

ANSWERS TO REVIEW TEST III ON PAGE 134.

He was one of the world's greatest artists. He was born in Greece but did most of his work in Spain. His religious paintings are haunting and original. His painting, "View of Toledo" is a brilliant landscape. He lived in the sixteenth century. The name of this great artist is <u>El Greco</u>.

She was the famous queen of the Nile. She was loved by Julius Caesar and lived with him in Rome. Later, she married Marc Antony and caused his downfall. She took her own life with the bite of a snake. She is a leading character in many great literary works. The name of this world famous person is <u>CLEOPATRA</u>.

ANSWERS TO SELF-TEST I ON PAGE 137.

1. ① 2   (clam   clan)

2. 1 ②   (tin   Tim)

3. ① 2   (bam   ban)

4. ① 2   (rum   run)

5. 1 ②   (sung   sum)

ANSWERS TO SELF-TEST I ON PAGE 140.

1. S Ⓓ   (It's the **sane** thing. It's the **same** thing.)

2. Ⓢ D   (Pick up the **phone**. Pick up the **phone**.)

3. S (D) (He is my **kin**. He is my **king**.)

4. (S) D (This is **fun**. This is **fun**.)

5. S (D) (Please don't **sin**. Please don't **sing**.)

ANSWERS TO SELF-TEST I ON PAGE 143.

1. 1 (2) She's a sinner. She's a *singer*.

2. (1) 2 It's not that *thing*. It's not that thin.

3. 1 (2) It's just a whim. It's just a *wing*.

4. (1) 2 I heard the *bang*. I heard the bam.

5. 1 (2) They had rum. They had *rung*.

ANSWERS TO SELF-TEST II ON PAGE 143.

1. (bring)	6. tangerine	11. (along)	16. engage
2. (anger)	7. (swing)	12. (talking)	17. (stinging)
3. (hang)	8. (tangle)	13. sponge	18. stingy
4. angel	9. danger	14. grin	19. lunch
5. (dancing)	10. (sink)	15. (running)	20. (bank)

ANSWERS TO SELF-TEST I ON PAGE 145.

1. thin	(thing)	6. seem	(scene)
2. (ban)	bang	7. (some)	sung
3. sinner	(singer)	8. (hammer)	hanger
4. (comb)	cone	9. ram	(rang)
5. rum	(run)	10. (gone)	gong

ANSWERS TO SELF-TEST II ON PAGE 145.

1. Jean sat in the _____ (sum (sun) sung).

2. The bird hurt his _____ (whim win (wing)).

3. It is fun to _____ (rum (run) rung).

4. The meat needs to _____ ((simmer) sinner singer).

5. They removed the _____ (bam (ban) band).

216 APPENDIX

ANSWERS TO SELF-TEST III ON PAGE 146.

1. I'll call ((them) then).
   [m]   [n]

2. He (ran (rang)) twice.
   [n] [ŋ]

3. That ((bun) bum) is old.
   [n] [m]

4. We got (some (sun)) at the beach.
   [m]   [n]

5. I heard a (bam (bang)).
   [m]   [ŋ]

6. You shouldn't ((sing) sin).
   [ŋ]   [n]

7. The children like (swinging (swimming)).
   [ŋ]   [m]

8. It's a small (ping (pin)).
   [ŋ]   [n]

9. Get rid of the ((gum) gun).
   [m]   [n]

10. Buy another (hammer (hanger)).
    [m]   [ŋ]

ANSWERS TO SELF-TEST IV ON PAGE 147.

	[n] [ŋ] [ŋ] [ŋ] [n] [n]
ANNOUNCER:	Is your skin feeling dry? Are you finding new wrinkles and lines? Then you
	[m] [n] [m] [n] [ŋ]
	need Pom's Skin Cream. Men and women everywhere are talking about our
	[n] [m] [m] [n] [ŋ]
	cream. Listen to famous film star Molly Malone who has been acting for a
	[ŋ] [ŋ] [ŋ]
	long, long, long time.
		[n] [n] [ŋ] [m] [n]
MOLLY:	Hmmmmm. Of course, everyone knows I started making films when I was
	[n] [ŋ] [ŋ]
	nine. But I've been using Pom's Cream for years and I think it's
	[n] [ŋ] [ŋ] [n]
	wonderful. Just put it on every morning and evening and in one week you'll
	[ŋ] [m] [n]
	start seeing the difference. Your face will gleam and shine and you'll look
	[n]
	just fine!

ANNOUNCER: And now for a limited time, you can get two jars for the price of one.
         [m]   [m]   [n]   [n]

Over *now for a limited time, you can get two jars for the price of one.*

        [m]   [m]   [n]   [m]   [m]

Remember, use Pom's Skin Cream and you too can look like a film star!

ANSWERS TO GENERAL REVIEW ACTIVITY I ON PAGE 149.

Other Words

1. nice	rice	twice	<u>mice</u>	[s]	(spice, lice, dice)
2. math	path	wrath	<u>bath</u>	[θ]	
3. trees	knees	seas	<u>bees</u>	[z]	(fees, he's, keys, peas)
4. patch	hatch	batch	<u>catch</u>	[tʃ]	(latch, match, scratch)
5. puff	rough	cuff	<u>buff</u>	[f]	(muff, stuff, scuff)
6. age	wage	stage	<u>cage</u>	[dʒ]	(page, rage, stage)
7. glove	of	dove	<u>love</u>	[v]	
8. baking	shaking	making	<u>taking</u>	[ŋ]	(faking, raking)
9. home	comb	foam	<u>dome</u>	[m]	(roam)
10. blessed	test	zest	<u>best</u>	[t]	(nest, pest, rest, west)

ANSWERS TO GENERAL REVIEW ACTIVITY II ON PAGE 149.

1. [s] ([z]) [θ] (zoo zero zipper)
2. ([ð]) [d] [t] (this that those)
3. [ʃ] ([tʃ]) [dʒ] (watch kitchen chair)
4. ([ʃ]) [j] [s] (shoe shirt fish)
5. [dʒ]([j]) [ŋ] (year yes yellow)

6. ([dʒ]) [j] [ʒ] (jam juice gem)
7. ([p]) [b] [v] (paper pet peas)
8. [b] ([v]) [f] (vest vote very)
9. ([m]) [n] [ŋ] (comb ham some)
10. [m] [n] ([ŋ]) (ring song think)

ANSWERS TO GENERAL REVIEW ACTIVITY III ON PAGE 150.

1. The bee**s** are bu**s**y bu**zz**ing in the flower**s**. [s] ([z]) [ð]

2. Nei**th**er fa**th**er nor mo**th**er have a bro**th**er. [θ] ([ð]) [d]

3. They are eati**ng** and drinki**ng** everythi**ng**. [n] [g] ([ŋ])

4. The tea**ch**er **ch**ose a ma**t**ure **ch**ild. [ʃ] ([tʃ]) [t]

5. My ne**ph**ew **F**rank is a **f**ine **ph**otographer. [v] ([f]) [p]

218 APPENDIX

ANSWERS TO GENERAL REVIEW ACTIVITY IV ON PAGE 150.

[tʃ]
An After-Dinner Speech

 [j]   [dʒ]   [t]   [ɪd]
A **Y**ale University **gra**d**u**ate was ask**ed** to speak at a dinner. He decid**ed** to speak about
           [ð]   [z]   [j]   [t]   [θ]   [h]
Yale. He said, "Yale, Y A L E. **Th**e Y stand**s** for **y**outh." He talk**ed** about **y**outh for **h**alf an
      [ð]   [ʃ]
hour. **Th**en he said, "The A stands for ambi**ti**on." He talked about ambition for an
      [ʒ]   [ŋ] [m]
unusually lo**ng** ti**m**e.
          [g]   [z]   [l]   [k]
The Yale **g**raduate then said, "The L repre**s**ents **l**oyalty." He spo**k**e about loyalty for
      [f]   [t]   [z]   [ʃ] [s]
almost an hour. **F**inally he reach**ed** E; he said "E stand**s** for effi**ci**en**c**y."
                [t] [f]   [m]   [w]
After he talked abou**t** e**ffi**ciency for a long ti**m**e he sat down. **O**ne man in the
     [s]   [t]   [ð]   [w]   [j] [θ] [v] [z]   [tʃ]   [p]
audien**c**e ask**ed** another man, "**W**hat do **y**ou **th**ink o**f** hi**s** spee**ch**?" The man replied, "I'm
[θ]   [ð]   [dʒ]   [tʃ]   [t]   [k]   [dʒ]
thankful **th**at he didn't **g**raduate from the Massa**ch**use**tt**s Institute of Te**ch**nolo**g**y!"

ANSWERS TO SELF-TEST I ON PAGE 155.

	2	3	1
1.	hot	hog	hop
	3	1	2
2.	wrote	rope	robe
	1	2	3
3.	save	safe	same
	3	2	1
4.	big	bid	bib
	1	3	2
5.	right	ride	ripe
	2	3	1
6.	mad	mat	map
	1	3	2
7.	fade	fate	fake
	3	1	2
8.	wipe	white	wife
	3	2	1
9.	peg	pen	pet
	2	1	3
10.	prize	prime	pride

ANSWERS TO SELF-TEST II ON PAGE 156.

1. The key opens the _____. ((lock) log lot)

2. The _____ is in the fire. (lock (log) lot)

3. _____ the dirty dishes. ((Soak) Soap Sole)

4. Wash your hands with _____. (soak (soap) sole)

5. He _____ the letter. ((wrote) rose rode)

6. He _____ the bicycle. (wrote rose (rode))

7. The _____ landed. (plague (plane) plate)

8. The _____ is broken. (plague plane (plate))

9. Send a birthday _____. (cart (card) carve)

10. The bags are in the _____. ((cart) card carve)

ANSWERS TO SELF-TEST III ON PAGE 157.

1. I can't find the ((belt) bell).

2. My son is (five (fine)).

3. I think he's ((dead) deaf).

4. Tim bought another (car (card)).

5. The (guild (guilt)) is ours.

6. The (pack (pact)) was sealed.

7. There's a ((lake) lane) near the house.

8. I (can (can't)) go.

9. The ((den) dent) is very small.

10. The ((colt) coal) is black.

ANSWERS TO SELF-TEST IV ON PAGE 157.

ANN: Hi, **Pam**! How was your **date** last **night** with **Pat**?

PAM: Nothing went **right** last **night**. **Pat** had a **flat** tire and came **late**!

ANN: How was the **food** at the **Old Inn**?

PAM: It was **bad**. The soup was **cold**. My **steak** was tough. They ran out of **chocolate cake**.

ANN: What about the dinner **Pat ate**?

PAM: His **duck** was over**done**. His **garlic bread** was **stale**!

ANN: Did it **cost** a lot of money?

PAM: Yes! and **Pat** didn't **have** enough to pay the **bill**.

ANN: I guess you **won't** go **out** with him **again**!

PAM: Why do you say **that**? We're going for a bike **ride** this afternoon. He's so **handsome**!

ANSWERS TO SELF-TEST I ON PAGE 162.

1. We (live (lived)) in Spain.

2. The stores ((open) opened) on Monday.

3. The farmers ((plant) planted) corn.

4. We (talk (talked)) about our problems.

5. The banks (loan (loaned)) money.

ANSWERS TO SELF-TEST II ON PAGE 163.

1. We ___danced___ the rumba and tango. [t]
2. She ___talked___ on the phone for an hour. [t]
3. Dad ___painted___ the fence green. [ɪd]
4. The student ___asked___ three quetsions. [t]
5. They ___waited___ 15 minutes for the bus. [ɪd]
6. I've ___lived___ in the same house for four years. [d]
7. My father ___mailed___ a letter. [d]
8. The man ___walked___ five miles. [t]
9. I ___deposited___ my check in the bank. [ɪd]
10. He ___washed___ his car with a hose. [t]

ANSWERS TO SELF-TEST III ON PAGE 163.

1. C (I) (Yesterday, I **shine** my shoes.)

2. C (I) (The children **watchid** [watʃɪd] TV.)

3. (C) I (Dad **rented** a car.)

4. C (I) (Who **call** you this morning?)

5. C (I) (John **cleant** [klint] his room.)

ANSWERS TO SELF-TEST IV ON PAGE 164.

1. (stopped)   started   stated

2. (finished)   followed   phoned

3. (loved)   looked   liked

4. tasted   traded   (taped)

5. cooked   (cleaned)   baked

6. packed   (pasted)   passed

7. ironed   sewed   (mended)

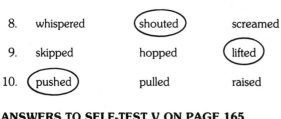

8.	whispered	(shouted)	screamed
9.	skipped	hopped	(lifted)
10.	(pushed)	pulled	raised

ANSWERS TO SELF-TEST V ON PAGE 165.

ROBERTA: Juanita, have you [ɪd] started your diet? I hope you haven't gained any weight. [d]

JUANITA: I boiled [d] eggs and sliced [t] celery for lunch.

ROBERTA: Have you exercised [d] at all?

JUANITA: I walked [t] five miles and jogged [d] in the park.

ROBERTA: Have you cleaned [d] the house? Calories can be worked [t] off!

JUANITA: I washed [t] and waxed [t] the floors. I even painted [ɪd] the bathroom.

ROBERTA: Who baked [t] this apple pie? Who cooked [t] this ham?

JUANITA: When I finished [t] cleaning I was starved. [d] I prepared [d] this food for dinner.

ROBERTA: Oh, no! I'll take this food home so you won't be tempted. [ɪd] I really enjoyed [d] being with you. Your diet is great!

JUANITA: What happened? [d] Somehow, I missed [t] out on all the fun.

ANSWERS TO SELF-TEST I ON PAGE 172.

1. The men cut the (tree (trees)).

2. He repaired the ((watch) watches).

3. The ((book) book's) cover is red.

4. Did they finally make (peace (peas)) ?

5. Did you see the little (cups (cubs)) ?

ANSWERS TO SELF-TEST II ON PAGE 172.

| 1. | talks | walks | (runs) |
| 2. | dishes | (gates) | pages |

3. pears   apples   (oranges)

4. eyes   (noses)   toes

5. (saves)   makes   cooks

6. newspapers   magazines   (books)

7. dogs   birds   (cats)

8. tables   chairs   (couches)

9. (dentists)   doctors   lawyers

10. lunches   beaches   (chimes)

ANSWERS TO SELF-TEST III ON PAGE 173.

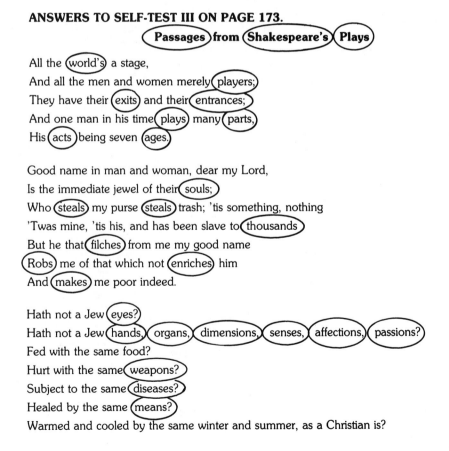

(Passages) from (Shakespeare's) (Plays)

All the (world's) a stage,
And all the men and women merely (players;)
They have their (exits) and their (entrances;)
And one man in his time (plays) many (parts,)
His (acts) being seven (ages.)

Good name in man and woman, dear my Lord,
Is the immediate jewel of their (souls;)
Who (steals) my purse (steals) trash; 'tis something, nothing
'Twas mine, 'tis his, and has been slave to (thousands)
But he that (filches) from me my good name
(Robs) me of that which not (enriches) him
And (makes) me poor indeed.

Hath not a Jew (eyes?)
Hath not a Jew (hands,) (organs,) (dimensions,) (senses,) (affections,) (passions?)
Fed with the same food?
Hurt with the same (weapons?)
Subject to the same (diseases?)
Healed by the same (means?)
Warmed and cooled by the same winter and summer, as a Christian is?

[s]	[z]	[ɪz]
exits	Shakespeare's	passages
parts	plays	entrances
acts	world's	ages
makes	players	filches
	souls	enriches
	steals	senses
	thousands	diseases
	robs	
	eyes	
	hands	
	organs	
	dimensions	
	affections	
	passions	
	weapons	
	means	

```
*************************************
```
SPANISH STUDY GUIDE
```
*************************************
```

AL ESTUDIANTE

Usted compró este programa porque sentía la necesidad de mejorar su pronunciación del inglés como segundo idioma. Sabemos que es muy frustrante que nos digan: "No puedo entenderle por su acento." También, sabemos el miedo que usted podría sentir al usar ciertas palabras y ser malentendido. Muchos de nuestros estudiantes tienen miedo de pronunciar palabras tales como: "sheet" y "beach." En su lugar usan "piece" y "ocean." No se preocupe, entendemos su problema y queremos ayudarle. Usted no tendrá que dejar de usar ciertas palabras o frases por temor a ser malentendido!

Este libro ha sido escrito para USTED. Muy pronto usted descubrirá que este programa ha sido diseñado para ayudarle a superar sus problemas de pronunciación al hablar inglés. Este es un programa independiente que usted podrá utilizar por su cuenta. El manual ha sido escrito con términos sencillos y fáciles de entender. El manual es acompañado de cintas magnetofónicas para ayudarle en la pronunciación de consonantes del inglés-americano. Usted no necesita una maestra (o terapista del habla) para usar este programa.

El manual contiene varios capítulos cubriendo las consonantes del idioma inglés. A cada capítulo le sigue un formato que contiene las siguientes secciones:

Pronunciando el Sonido

En esta sección se da una explicación sencilla de cómo se pronuncia el sonido. Se dan detalles de la posición de los articuladores (labios, lengua, etc.).

Palabras Claves en Español

En esta sección, se dan palabras claves en español que contienen la consonante equivalente en inglés. Estas palabras le darán un sonido familiar que usted podrá asociar.

Posibles Problemas de Pronunciación para Personas de Habla Hispana

En esta sección se le explica porqué la pronunciación de las consonantes en inglés son problemáticas para usted y cómo estas difieren de la pronunciación de las consonantes en español.

Sugerencias

Esta sección contiene una serie de reglas que le ayudarán a pronunciar el sonido. Estas reglas han sido diseñadas para ayudarle a usar los patrones de deletreo como guía de pronunciación.

Ejercicios

Esta sección consiste de una serie de ejercicios diseñados para darle práctica con los sonidos de las consonantes tal y cómo ocurren en las palabras, frases comunes y oraciones.

Exámenes

Esta sección incluye una variedad de exámenes breves diseñados para que usted se dé cuenta del progreso que ha tenido. Se examinará su capacidad para reconocer y pronunciar el sonido en palabras, oraciones y conversación.

Para un "Encore" . . .

Esta sección ha sido diseñada con el propósito de que usted use la consonante clave en situaciones del diario vivir. Una serie de actividades de escuchar, lectura y conversación se incluyen al final de cada capítulo.

Las cintas magnetofónicas que acompañan el manual contienen secciones de cada capítulo (están claramente marcadas en el manual) y han sido diseñadas para proveer un modelo correcto de pronunciación para cada sonido. Favor de referirse a la página vii para un esquema del material que se incluye en las cintas.

Como Usar el Programa

Ahora usted está listo para comenzar el programa. Los únicos materiales que necesitará serán: una grabadora para las cintas y un espejo que le ayude a colocar los articuladores al hacer un sonido. Busque un lugar tranquilo y cómodo donde practicar: Llénese de entusiasmo y determinación de que mejorará su pronunciación—¡y usted estará listo para empezar!!

Antes de comenzar el programa, lea el capítulo 1 en el manual y toque la cinta 1 (lado A) para familiarizarse con el formato de las lecciones. (Asegúrese que entiende las explicaciones en el manual antes de empezar las prácticas orales.)

Ejercicios

Renueve la marcha de la cinta al comienzo y mire el ejercicio A, capítulo 1 (página 12). Practique el ejercicio como le indican las direcciones. Repita las palabras después del instructor, durante las pausas. Usted puede parar la cinta cuando usted desee repetir una sección. Si usted tiene dificultad en algún momento, pare la cinta, y repase las instrucciones de pronunciación de la consonante. Revise el espejo y asegúrese que sus articuladores están en la posición correcta. Continue de esta misma manera con cada ejercicio hasta que usted esté seguro de que puede decir las palabras y oraciones con facilidad. Antes de comenzar la próxima sección, repita el material despues del instructor sin mirar el libro.

Exámenes

Una vez se sienta seguro de que puede hacer los ejercicios, comienze con las pruebas o exámenes. Las instrucciones para cada examen varían: así que, lea cada una de ellas cuidadosamente antes de empezar. Al terminar cada examen, apague la grabadora y revise las respuestas en el apéndice. Si usted tiene alguna dificultad con los exámenes, regrese al principio del capítulo y repita los ejercicios. Las partes de más dificultad son los diálogos y los párrafos, repáselos varias veces a medida que va progresando en el manual.

Para un "Encore" . . .

Cuando se sienta satisfecho con la pronunciación de una consonante específica, usted está listo para pasar del libro a las situaciones del diario vivir. Estas son sugerencias para automatizar el proceso de pronunciación. Trate de buscar otras maneras de incorporar el sonido aprendido a su rutina diaria.

Repaso de Capítulos

El repaso de çapítulos ha sido diseñado para darle a usted práctica adicional. Termine los exámenes como hizo en los capítulos anteriores. Si tiene problema con algunas de las consonantes, regrese al capítulo y repáselo.

Sesiones de Práctica

Es muy importante practicar. Trate de hacer una rutina del tiempo que dedica a estos estudios. Lo ideal es practicar diariamente, pero si su tiempo es corto, practique por lo menos de 3 a 4 veces a la semana (por 20–30 minutos). Sabemos que leer un libro y oir cintas es un trabajo muy arduo y dificil.

Tómese un descanso cuando se sienta cansado. Continue su sesión de estudio cuando se sienta fresco y descansado. ¡NO TRATE DE HACERLO TODO DE UNA VEZ! *El perfeccionamiento toma tiempo. Pero poco a poco usted llegará lejos.*

Mantenga la grabadora y las cintas cerca de su area de trabajo, ya sea en la cocina o en el auto. Lo importante es practicar cuando se sienta relajado, descansado y motivado, así, lo hará lo mejor posible sin mucho esfuerzo. *¡RECUERDE, QUE LA PRÁCTICA ES LO QUE NOS LLEVA A LA PERFECCIÓN!!!*

Otras Maneras de Mejorar su Pronunciación

Escuchar es una manera de mejorar la pronunciación. Aproveche el mayor número de oportunidades para escuchar hablar inglés. Puede hacerlo siguiendo estas sugerencias:

1. Mire las noticias en la televisión. Preste atención a la pronunciación del locutor. Repita algunas de las palabras o frases que el dice en voz alta. (*No se preocupe, su familia no pensará que está hablando solo! Le admirarán pues saben que usted esta tratando de mejorar su pronunciación!*)

2. Oiga las noticias en la radio de 5 a 10 minutos. Repita algunas de las palabras o frases del locutor. (*Si las personas le miran de manera extraña porque creen que usted está loco, dígale que está practicando su pronunciación!*)

3. Cuando su programa de televisión favorito comienze, trate de entender el diálogo sin mirar la pantalla. *Pero*, si tiene que mirar la pantalla para entenderlo, entonces espere los comerciales para practicar la destreza de escuchar.

4. Converse frecuentemente con alguien nativo del idioma inglés-americano.

5. Pregúntele al que le está escuchando si su pronunciación ha sido correcta. *Ellos se sentirán felices de poderle ayudar!*

6. **Pero lo mas importante de todo—SEA VALIENTE!** Los ejercicios están llenos de expresiones comunes. Use algunas de ellas en su conversación diaria como parte de su tarea.

Aunque este programa tiene como énfasis la pronunciación, el material incluido en el manual es de gran ayuda para su vocabulario. Cuando no entienda una frase o expresión idiomática, búsquela en el diccionario. Escriba la definición en el manual y así no se le olvidará.

Usted se preguntará cuanto tiempo le tomará para notar una mejoría. Nosotros creemos que el curso provee todo lo que usted necesita para mejorar su pronunciación. Si usted sigue el programa en el orden indicado, usted notará una mejoría en un par de semanas. *Recuerde que mientras más practique, mas rápida será su mejoría!*

La motivación es un factor que puede contribuir enormemente. Muchos actores y actrices han tenido que perder el acento para poderse convertir en artistas de cine. No le podemos garantizar un contrato en el cine, pero sí podemos garantizarle que este programa le ayudará a que sea entendido y se comunique mejor en la vida cotidiana. **¡Buena suerte!**

¡Vire la página, y vamos a comenzar!

DEFINICIONES

A medida que vaya avanzando en este manual, usted verá frecuentemente los términos *encía, paladar blando, aspiración, consonante sonora, consonante sorda,* y *articuladores*. Ahora le vamos a definir estos términos.

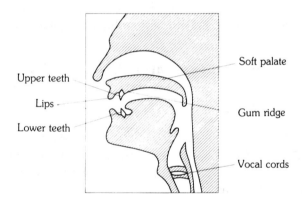

ENCIA ALVEOLAR: La encía alveolar es la parte dura del cielo de su boca, la cual está justamente detrás de sus dientes superiores y delanteros.

PALADAR BLANDO: El paladar blando es la parte suave y movible de la porción trasera del cielo de su boca.

ASPIRACION: Aspiración se refiere a la acción de producir un sonido con un soplo de respiración. En inglés, ciertas consonantes ([p], [t], [k], y [h]) son sonidos "aspirados." Deben de ser producidos con un soplo fuerte de aire.

CONSONANTE SONORA: Una consonante sonora es un sonido producido cuando las cuerdas vocales están vibrando. Coloque la mano en su garganta sobre las cuerdas vocales mientras tararea, y usted podrá sentir las vibraciones de las cuerdas vocales al decir **"mmmmmmmmmmmmmm."**

CONSONANTE SORDA: Una consonante sorda es un sonido producido sin vibraciones de las cuerdas vocales. Coloque sus manos sobre las cuerdas vocales y produzca el siseo **"ssssss."** Esta vez, no sentirá vibración ninguna!

ARTICULADORES: Los articuladores son las distintas partes de la la boca que usamos cuando hablamos tales como los labios, la lengua, el paladar blando, los dientes y la quijada.

Los sonidos de las consonantes variadas son creados por:

1. **La posición de sus articuladores.** Por ejemplo, la punta de la lengua debe tocar el borde de la encía alveolar para decir sonidos como [t], [d], [n], o [l], pero debe sobresalir entre los dientes para decir [θ] como en *"think"* (pensar) or [ð] como en *"them"* (ellos).

2. **La manera que la corriente de aire sale de la boca o nariz.** Por ejemplo, la corriente de aire o respiración es contínua para las consonantes [s] o [f] pero es parada completamente y luego estallada para la [p] o la [t].

3. **La vibración de las cuerdas vocales.** Por ejemplo, las cuerdas vocales no vibran con los sonidos [s], [f], o [t], pero debe añadir "sonoridad" con los sonidos [z], [v], o [d].

El cuadro debajo categoriza las consonantes sonoras y sordas. ¡No trate de memorizar este cuadro! Coloque sus manos sobre las cuerdas vocales al decir los sonidos siguientes. Usted podrá oir y **"sentir"** la diferencia entre consonantes sonoras y sordas.

SONORAS	SORDAS
[b]	[p]
[d]	[t]
[g]	[k]
[v]	[f]
[z]	[s]
[ð]	[θ]
[ʤ]	[tʃ]
[ʒ]	[ʃ]
[m], [n], [ŋ]	[h]
[j], [w], [l], [r]	

PRONUNCIANDO [s] COMO EN "SIT" (Page 11)

La Punta de la Lengua:	está cerca pero no toca la encía alveolar detrás de los dientes superiores y delanteros
La Corriente de Aire:	es continua y sin interrupción
Las Cuerdas Vocalas:	no están vibrando

El sonido [s] en inglés es producido de la misma manera que las letras "s" y "z" en español.

Posibles Problemas de Pronunciación Para Personas de Habla Hispana

El sonido [s] es un sonido común en español y debe ser fácil de decir para usted. Sin embargo, cuando la vocal "e" precede la [s] en muchas palabras: (escuela, estudiante, espanol). Es muy probable que usted pronuncie incorrectamente la "e" antes de la [s] en inglés. Ejemplos:

Si usted produce la "e" antes de la [s]:

state	(estado)	sonará como	**estate**	(propriedad)
say	(decir)	sonará como	**essay**	(ensayo)
steam	(vapor)	sonará come	**esteem**	(estimación)

Al decir la [s], mantenga la corriente de aire constante como el "siseo" de una serpiente (sssssss)! Acuérdese, en español es "escuela" y "estudiar" pero en inglés es "school" y "study."

PRONUNCIANDO [z] COMO EN "ZOO" (Page 14)

La Lengua:	en la misma posición que la [s].
La Corriente de Aire:	es continua y sin interrupción
Las Cuerdas Vocales:	están vibrando

En muchos dialectos del español, cuando la letra "s" es seguida por una consonante sonora (m, l, d, g), esta es pronunciada como una [z]. (Ejemplos: *mismo, isla, desde, rasgar.*)

Posibles Problemas de Pronunciación Para Personas de Habla Hispana

El sonido [z] no es un sonido común en español. Posiblemente, usted pronuncia la letra "z" en inglés de la misma manera que en español (como [s]).

Tambien, los patrones irregulares de deletreo en inglés contribuyen a su problema con esta consonante. Ejemplos: Si usted dice [s] en vez de [z]:

zoo (zoologico)　sonará como **Sue** (nombre próprio)
eyes (ojos)　sonará como **ice** (hielo)
prize (premio)　sonará como **price** (precio)

Acuérdese, [z] es un sonido sonoro. Sus cuerdas vocales deben vibrar o por error dirá [s]. Piense en el zumbido de la abeja (**bzzzzzzzz**) y dirá sus **"Zetas"** con facilidad!

PRONUNCIANDO [t] COMO EN "TOP" (Page 23)

La Punta de la Lengua:　está oprimiendo firmemente la encía alveolar, detrás de los dientes superiores y delanteros
La Corriente de Aire:　es parada y luego estallada
Las Cuerdas Vocales:　no están vibrando

El sonido [t] en inglés es similar al sonido de la letra "t" en español. (La [t] en inglés es aspirada y producida con un soplo fuerte de aire.)

Posibles Problemas de Pronunciación
Para Personas de Habla Hispana

El sonido [t] es una consonante familiar para usted. Sin embargo, la [t] es mucho mas explosiva en inglés que en español. Al hablar inglés, la punta de su lengua debe tocar la encía alveolar y no la parte trasera de sus dientes superiores y delanteros. La [t] debe de ser dicha con una aspiración fuerte y un soplo de aire o sino sonará como la [d].

Practique diciendo la [t] mientras aguanta un papel delante de su boca. Si usted correctamente aspira la [t] y la dice con un soplo de aire, su papel ondeará.

*Cuando la "t" está en medio de dos vocales (como en "water" ⟨**agua**⟩**, "butter"** ⟨**mantequilla**⟩**, "city"** ⟨**ciudad**⟩**, etc.) no es aspirada. La "t" en medio de sonidos de vocales suena como la "r" en español de las palabras "caro, pero, moro."**
Cuando la "t" sigue la "s" (como en "stop" ⟨parar**⟩**, "stay"** ⟨**quedarse**⟩**, "stick"** ⟨**palo**⟩**, etc.) NO es aspirada con un soplo de aire.**

PRONUNCIANDO [d] COMO EN "DAY" (Page 28)

La Punta de la Lengua: está oprimida firmemente detras de los dientes delanteros y superiores.

La Corriente de Aire: es parada y luego estallada

Las Cuerdas Vocales: están vibrando

El sonido [d] en inglés es similar al sonido de la letra "d" al comienzo de una palabra o cuando sigue a la "n" o la "l" en español.

Posibles Problemas de Pronunciación Para Personas de Habla Hispana

1. El sonido [d] debe de producirse con la punta de la lengua tocando la encía alveolar, y no la parte trasera de sus dientes delanteros y superiores, tampoco debe de producirse con la punta de la lengua colocado entre sus dientes como en muchas palabras en español. Si no toca la encia alveolar cuando dice la [d], esto contribuirá a no mejorar su acento. Incluso podrá sonar como la [ð]: Ejemplos:

   Si usted dice [ð] en vez de decir [d]:

ladder	(escalera)	sonará como	**lather**	(espuma)
breeding	(crianza)	sonará como	**breathing**	(respirando)

2. Cuando la [d] es el ultimo sonido en una palabra, muchas personas de habla hispana olvidan que las cuerdas vocales deben vibrar. Esto hará que el sonido [d] suene como la [t] y podría confundir a sus oyentes. Ejemplos:

   Si usted dice [t] en vez de decir [d]:

card	(tarjeta)	sonará como	**cart**	(carreta)
bed	(cama)	sonará como	**bet**	(apuesta)

Su [d] sería perfecta si oprime la punta de la lengua en la encía alveolar detrás de sus dientes delanteros y superiores y asi añadir sonoridad.

PRONUNCIANDO [θ] COMO EN "THINK" (Page 32)

La Punta de la Lengua: está colocada entre los dientes

La Corriente de Aire: es continua y sin interrupción

Las Cuerdas Vocales: no están vibrando

El sonido [θ] es similar al "Ceceo castellano" usado por los *"madrileños"* al pronunciar palabras como "hace" y "zapato." (Las letras "c" y "z" son pronunciades con la lengua entre los dientes.)

Posibles Problemas de Pronunciación
Para Personas de Habla Hispana

El sonido [θ] no existe en la mayoría de los dialectos en español. Tal véz le sea dificil reconocer este sonido y usted posiblemente lo sustituya por sonidos mas familiares. Ejemplos:

Si usted sustituye la [s] por la [θ]:

thank   (dar gracias)   sonará como   **sank**   (hundir)
thing   (cosa)   sonará como   **sing**   (cantar)

Si usted sustituye [t] por la [θ]:

path   (camino) sonará como   **pat**   (palmadita)

El sonido [θ] le será facil de pronunciar si usted se concentra en colocar su lengua entre sus dientes, (MIRESE EN EL ESPEJO!) y trate de que la corriente de aire sea continua.

PRONUNCIANDO [ð] COMO EN "THE" (Page 37)

La Punta de la Lengua: está colocada entre los dientes
La Corriente de Aire: es continua y sin interrupcíon
Las Cuerdas Vocales: están vibrando

El sonido [ð] en inglés es similar al sonido de la letra "d" en medio de vocales de ciertas palabras en español. (En actualidad, [ð] es mas fuerte y mas visible entre los dientes.)

Posibles Problemas de Pronunciación
Para Personas de Habla Hispana

El sonido [ð] no existe ni al principio ni al final de palabras en español. Este sonido puede que sea dificil para usted de reconocer y producir. Usted seguramente lo sustituya con un sonido más familiar de la [d]. Ejemplos:

Si usted sustituye [d] por [ð]:

they	(ellos)	sonará como	**day**	(día)
lather	(espuma)	sonará como	**ladder**	(escalera)
breathe	(respirar)	sonará como	**breed**	(cría)

Cuando pronuncia [ð], acuérdese de colocar la lengua entre sus dientes y de mantener la corriente de aire continua en su boca. Mire al espejo mientras practica sus ejercicios de la [ð].

PRONUNCIANDO [ʃ] COMO EN "SHOE" (Page 47)

La Punta de la Lengua: se aproxima pero no toca la encía alveolar
El Medio de la Lengua: se approxima pero no toca el paladar duro
La Corriente de Aire: es continua y sin interrupción
Las Cuerdas Vocales: no están vibrando

Posibles Problemas de Pronunciación
Para Personas de Habla Hispana

La consonante [ʃ] no existe en español. Usted seguramente la sustituya por un sonido más familiar de la [tʃ] (el sonido que será explicado en la sección siguiente). Ejemplos:

Si usted sustituye [tʃ] por [ʃ]:

shoe	(zapato)	sonará como	**chew**	(masticar)
wash	(lavar)	sonará como	**watch**	(observar)

El sonido [ʃ] le será fácil de pronunciar si usted mantiene la corriente de aire firme y suave. Tenga cuidado y no deje que su lengua toque sus dientes ni encía alveolar o dirá [tʃ] por error.

PRONUNCIANDO [tʃ] COMO EN "CHAIR" (Page 50)

La Punta de la Lengua: está firmamente oprimiendo la encía alveolar detras de los dientes superiores y delanteros
La Corriente de Aire: es parada (como para la [t] y luego soltada (como para la [ʃ].
Las Cuerdas Vocales: no están vibrando

El sonido de [tʃ] es similar al sonido de la letra "ch" en español. Empieza como la consonante [t] y termina como la consonante [ʃ].

Posibles Problemas de Pronunciación
Para Personas de Habla Hispana

Aunque [tʃ] es un sonido familar en español, este podría confundirse facilmente con el sonido [ʃ] del inglés. Ejemplos:

Si usted dice [ʃ] en vez de [tʃ]:

chair	(silla)	sonará como	***share***	(compartir)
which	(cual)	sonará como	***wish***	(deseo)

Nada mas acuérdese de empezar [tʃ] con su lengua en el mismo lugar que
el sonido [t]. Asegúrese de oprimir la punta de su lengua contra la encía
alveolar detrás de sus dientes superiores y delanteros, o sino dirá [ʃ] por error.
La [tʃ] es un sonido explosivo como un estornudo.

PRONUNCIANDO [ʒ] COMO EN "MEASURE" (Page 58)

La Lengua: está en la misma posición que [ʃ]
La Corriente de Aire: es continua y sin interrupción
Las Cuerdas Vocales: están vibrando

El sonido [ʒ] existe en el español de la Argentina, el Uruguay, y del centro
de Colombia. En estos paises, las letras "y" y "ll" del español son pronunciadas como [ʒ] en palabras como "yo" y "llamar."

Posibles Problemas de Pronunciación
Para Personas de Habla Hispana

En sonido [ʒ] no existe en la mayoría de los dialectos del español. Sus problemas de pronunciación posiblemente ocurren por la semejanza entre [ʒ] y
[ʃ]. Ejemplos:

Si usted sustituye [ʃ] por [ʒ]:

vision	(visión)	sonará como	**"vishion"**
beige	(color crema)	sonará como	**"beish"**

Asegurese de que sus cuerdas vocales vibren cuando dice [ʒ] o sino usted lo
sustituirá con [ʃ]. (Póngase las manos sobre su garganta; sienta la vibración.)

PRONUNCIANDO [ʤ] COMO EN "JAW" (Page 63)

La Punta de la Lengua:	está oprimiendo firmemente la encía alveolar detrás de los dientes superiores y delanteros
La Corriente de Aire:	es parada (como para la [d] y luego soltado (como para la [ʒ])
Las Cuerdas Vocales:	están vibrando

El sonido [ʤ] existe en la mayoría de los dialectos del español cuando las letras "y" y "ll" empiezan la primera palabra de una oración. El uso de [ʤ] es evidente particularmente en el español de Chile, Paraguay, Puerto Rico, la Republica Dominicana, y partes de Cuba y Bolivia.

Posibles Problemas de Pronunciación
Para Personas de Habla Hispana

Confusión con patrones de deletrear en inglés y la semenjanza entre [j] y otros sonidos causan problema de pronunciación con [ʤ]. Ejemplos:

Si usted sustituye [j] por [d]:

    Jello   (gelatina)   sonará como   ***yellow***   (amarillo)

Si usted sustituye [h] por [d]:

    jam   (jalea)   sonará como   ***ham***   (jamón)

Simplemente acuérdese de empezar [ʤ] con su lengua en el mismo lugar que el sonido de la [d]. Asegúrese que su lengua este oprimida en contra de la encía alveolar, y de que sus cuerdas vocales estén vibrando cuando diga [ʤ].

PRONUNCIANDO [j] AS IN "YOU" (Page 67)

La Lengua:	está en la misma posición que la vocal [i]
La Corriente de Aire:	es continua y sin interrupción
Las Cuerdas Vocales:	están vibrando

La consonante [j] en inglés es similar al sonido de las letras "y," "ll," e "hie" en muchos de los dialectos del español.

Posibles Problemas de Pronunciación
Para Personas de Habla Hispaña

En muchos dialectos del español, los oradores varían en el uso de los sonidos [j] y [ʤ]. En inglés, estos sonidos no pueden intercambiarse sin confundir a su oyente. Ejemplos:

Si usted dice [ʤ] en vez de [j]:

yet	(todavía)	sonará como	**jet**	(avión de chorro)
you	(usted)	sonará como	**Jew**	(judío)

Para pronunciar [j] correctamente, asegúrese de que la punta de la lengua está opuesta a la parte trasera de los dientes inferiores y delanteros y no tocando el cielo de la boca. Acuérdese de las palabras claves en español: pollo, vaya, hierba.

PRONUNCIANDO [p] COMO EN "PAY" (Page 81)

Los Labios: se oprimen juntos
La Corriente de Aire: es parada y luego estallada
Las Cuerdas Vocales: no están vibrando

El sonido [p] en inglés es similar al sonido de la "p" en español. (La [p] en inglés es mucho mas aspirada y está producida con un soplo de aire más fuerte.)

Posibles Problemas de Pronunciación
Para Personas de Habla Hispana

Esta consonante es familiar para usted. Pero, la [p] es mucho mas explosiva en inglés que en español. Al hablar inglés la [p] debe de producirse aspirando fuertemente y con un soplo de aire o tal vez suene como una [b]. Ejemplos:

Si se le olvida aspirar la [p]:

pear	(pera)	sonará como	**bear**	(oso)
pat	(palmadita)	sonará como	**bat**	(bate)

Practique diciendo la [p] mientras aguanta un papel delante de los labios. Si aspira la [p] correctamente y lo dice con un soplo de aire, el papel ondeará.

*Cuando la [p] sigue la [s] (como en "spot" ⟨mancha⟩, "spend" ⟨gastar⟩, "spy" ⟨espiar⟩, etc.), no es aspirada con un soplo de aire.

PRONUNCIANDO [b] COMO EN "BOY" (Page 85)

Los Labios: se oprimen juntos (como para [p])
La Corriente de Aire: es parada y luego estallada
Las Cuerdas Vocales: están vibrando

La consonante [b] en inglés es similar al sonido de la letra "b"' cuando sigue a "n" o "m" o cuando empieza una oración en español.

Posibles Problemas de Pronunciación Para Personas de Habla Hispana

1. Las letras "b" y "v" en español son pronunciadas iguales frecuentemente. En inglés usted puede confundir estos dos sonidos. Ejemplos:

   Si usted usa [v] en vez de [b]:

   boat (barco) sonará como **vote** (votar)

2. Cuando [b] es el último sonido en una palabra, a muchas personas de habla hispana se les olvida vibrar las cuerdas vocales. Esto hace que [b] suene como [p] en vez de [b]. Ejemplos:

   Si usted dice [p] en vez de [b]:

   robe (bata) sonará como **rope** (soga)
   cab (coche) sonará como **cap** (gorra)

   La consonante [b] le será facil de decir si usted hace que las cuerdas vocales vibren y los labios se opriman firmamente.

PRONUNCIANDO [f] COMO EN "FUN" (Page 89)

Los Dientes Superiores: tocan el labio inferior
La Corriente de Aire: es continua y sin interrupción
Las Cuerdas Vocales: no están vibrando

El sonido [f] es pronunciado de la misma manera que la letra "f" en español.

Posibles Problemas de Pronunciación
Para Personas de Habla Hispana

Este es un sonido familiar en español y no debe de causarle ninguna dificultad en inglés. Piense en la palabra clave del español *café* y la [f] le quedará perfectamente bien!

PRONUNCIANDO [v] COMO EN "VERY" (Page 93)

Los Dientes Superiores: tocan al labio inferior (como para la [f])
La Corriente de Aire: es continua y sin interrupción
Las Cuerdas Vocales: están vibrando

La consonante [v] no existe en la mayoría de los dialectos del español.

Posibles Problemas de Pronunciación
Para Personas de Habla Hispana

1. La letra "v" en español es pronunciada como la "b" (*tuvo y tubo* son pronunciadas de la misma manera). Por lo tanto, usted probablemente sustituya [b] por [v] al hablar inglés. Esto confundirá muchísimo a sus oyentes. Ejemplos:

   Si usted dice [b] en vez de [v]:

   very   (muy)   sonará como   **berry**   (baya)
   vest   (chaleco)   sonará como   **best**   (mejor)

2. Cuando la [v] es el último sonido en una palabra, muchas personas de habla hispana olvidan vibrar sus cuerdas vocales. Esto hará que el sonido de la [v] suene como [f] y confunda a sus oyentes. Ejemplos:

   Si usted dice [f] en vez de [v]:

   save   (ahorrar)   sonará como   **safe**   (salvado)
   leave   (irse)   sonará como   **leaf**   (hoja)

El sonido de la [v] le será facil de pronunciar si se concentra en colocar sus dientes superiores sobre sus labios inferiores. Mire al espejo mientras practica los ejercicios de la [v] y acuérdese de vibrar sus cuerdas vocales.

PRONUNCIANDO [k] COMO EN "CAKE" (Page 103)

La Parte Trasera de la Lengua: toca el paladar blando
La Corriente de Aire: es parada y luego explotada
Las Cuerdas Vocales: no están vibrando

El sonido de la [k] en inglés es similar al sonido de las letras "c" y "k" en ciertas palabras del español. (La [k] en inglés es aspirada y producida con un soplo de aire fuerte.)

Posibles Problemas de Pronunciación
Para Personas de Habla Hispana

Esta es una consonante facil de pronunciar para usted. Nada más que acuérdese que la [k] es mas explosiva en inglés que en español. Debe de decirse con aspiración fuerte y un soplo de aire.*

*Cuando [k] sigue a [s] (como en "sky" ⟨cielo⟩, "skin" ⟨piel⟩, "skate" ⟨patinar⟩), no es aspirada con un soplo de aire.

PRONUNCIANDO [g] COMO EN "GO" (Page 107)

La Parte Trasera de la Lengua: toca el paladar blando
La Corriente de Aire: es parada y luego estallada
Las Cuerdas Vocales: están vibrando

El sonido [g] en inglés es similar al sonido de la letra "g" en español despues de "n" o antes de *a, o, u,* o *r,* en ciertas palabras en español. (La [g] en inglés es mas explosiva que en español.)

Posibles Problemas de Pronunciación
Para Personas de Habla Hispana

Esta es otra consonante facil de pronunciar para usted. Pero, cuando la [g] es el último sonido en una palabra, quizas se le olvide añadir sonoridad. Esto hará que el sonido [g] suene como [k] y cambie el significado de su palabra. Ejemplos:
Si usted sustituye [k] por [g]:

bag	(bolsa)	sonará como	**back**	(espalda)
dug	(excavo)	sonará como	**duck**	(pato)

Siempre vibre sus cuerdas vocales para la [g] especialmente al final de las palabras. Deje ir a su [g] con una explosión.

PRONUNCIANDO [w] COMO EN "WE" (Page 111)

Los Labios: son redondeados y en la misma posición que la vocal [u]

La Corriente de Aire: es continua

Las Cuerdas Vocales: están vibrando

El sonido [w] es similar al sonido de las letras "u" en español despues de *c, g, o b* (como en "cuando," "antiguo," "abuela"), o "hu" (huele, hueso) en muchos de los dialectos de español.

Posibles Problemas de Pronunciación
Para Personas de Habla Hispana

El sonido [w] frecuentemente es intercambiado por la [g] en muchos dialectos del español. Por ejemplo, algunos oradores dicen frecuentemente [gueso] o [weso] al decir "hueso." Si usted pronuncia el sonido [w] del inglés de una manera fuerte y aspera como lo hacen muchas personas de habla hispana al decir "hu," este sonará como si usted estuviera diciendo una [g] antes de [w]. Ejemplos:

Si usted dice [g] antes de [w]:

      want   (querer)   sonará como   **"gwant"**
      when   (cuando)   sonará como   **"gwen"**

Acuérdese de redondear sus labios al decir [w]. Usted debe de sentir todos los movimientos del habla en la parte delantera de su boca, y no en la parte trasera.

PRONUNCIANDO [l] COMO EN "LAMP" (Page 116)

La Punta de la Lengua: es oprimida contra la encía alveolar detras de los dientes superiores y delanteros

La Corriente de Aire: es contínua y pasa por ambos lados de la lengua

Las Cuerdas Vocales: están vibrando

El sonido [l] en inglés es similar al sonido de la letra "l" en español.

Posibles Problemas de Pronunciación
Para Personas de Habla Hispana

Este es un sonido familiar en español y no debe de causarle ninguna dificultad en inglés.

PRONUNCIANDO [r] COMO EN "RED" (Page 120)

La Punta de la Lengua: se riza hacía arriba sin tocar el cielo de la boca
La Corriente de Aire: es continua
Las Cuerdas Vocales: están vibrando

Posibles Problemas de Pronunciación
Para Personas de Habla Hispana

La manera de pronunciar el sonido de la [r] en inglés no existe en español. La "r" en español vibra mientras la punta de la lengua toca la encía alveolar una o mas veces. Probablemente, usted use la "r" del español al hablar inglés. Esto no cambiará el significado de las palabras pero contribuirá a un "acento muy fuerte."

    Asegúrese que su lengua no toque la encía alveolar y usted pronunciará correctamente la [r] en inglés.

PRONUNCIANDO [h] COMO EN "HAT" (Page 124)

La Lengua: se desliza para adoptar la posición de la vocal que le sigue a la [h]
La Corriente de Aire: es continua
Las Cuerdas Vocales: no están vibrando

El sonido [h] es similar al sonido de la "g" en español antes de la "e" o "i" (como en "gente" y "girar"), y de la "j" (jota) en varios dialectos del español. El uso de la [h] es mas evidente en el español de Centro America, El Caribe, Colombia, y Venezuela.

Posibles Problemas de Pronunciación
Para Personas de Habla Hispana

1. La letra "h" del español es muda. Por lo tanto, personas de habla hispana a veces omiten este sonido en inglés. Ejemplos:

   Si usted omite la [h]:

hat	(sombrero)	sonará como	**at**	(en)
hand	(mano)	sonará como	**and**	(y)

2. Ya que quizas no exista la [h] en su dialecto del español, usted tal vez la pronuncie de una manera fuerte y áspera como lo hacen muchas personas de habla hispana al decir la "g" o "j." Este es un sonido fácil de pronunciar.

Relaje su garganta y lengua; suavemente deje salir un soplo de aire como si estuviera suspirando!

PRONUNCIANDO [m] COMO EN "ME" (Page 135)

Los Labios: están juntos en posición para 'tararear'
La Corriente de Aire: es continua por la naríz
Las Cuerdas Vocales: están vibrando

El sonido [m] es pronunciado como la letra "m" del español.

Posibles Problemas de Pronunciación
Para Personas de Habla Hispana

Este es un sonido familiar para usted; le será fácil de pronunciar al principio y en el medio de las palabras. Quizas sustituya [n] o [ŋ], sonidos mas familiares al final de las palabras en inglés. Ejemplos:

Si usted dice [n] en vez de [m]:

> **some** (algunos) se convierte en **sun**   (sol)
> **swim** (nadar)   se convierte en **swing** (columpios)

Acuérdese de llevar sus labios a una posición para "tararear" al decir [m].

PRONUNCIANDO [n] COMO EN "NO" (Page 137)

La Lengua: esta oprimida firmemente contra la encía alveolar
                            detras de los dientes superiores y delanteros
La Corriente de Aire: es continua por la naríz
Las Cuerdas Vocales: están vibrando

Posibles Problemas de Pronunciación
Para Personas de Habla Hispana

Las personas de habla hispana frecuentemente confunden por su semejanza las consonantes nasales [m], [n], y [ŋ] al final de las palabras en inglés. Ejemplos:

Si usted dice [m] en vez de [n]:

> **sun** (sol)   sonará como **some** (algunos)
> **ran** (corrió)   sonará como **rang** (sono)

Siempre oprima firmamente su lengua contra la encía alveolar detrás de los dientes superiores y delanteros, en especial al final de las palabras.

PRONUNCIANDO [ŋ] COMO EN "SING" (Page 140)

La Parte Trasera de la Lengua: se eleva en contra del paladar blando
La Corriente de Aire: es continua por la naríz
Las Cuerdas Vocales: están vibrando

El sonido [ŋ] existe en español cuando la letra "n" es seguida por "g," "c," o "j" (cangrejo, encantar, un juego). En muchos dialectos del español, en particular en el de Cuba, la Republica Dominicana, y Centro America, la "n" al final de palabras es pronunciada [ŋ] (pan = [pɑŋ]).

Posibles Problemas de Pronunciación
Para Personas de Habla Hispana

Muchas personas de habla hispana no están acostumbradas a pronunciar [ŋ] al final de las palabras. Tambien la semejanza entre [ŋ] y [n] los podría confundir. Ejemplos:
Si usted dice [n] en vez de [ŋ]:

feeling (sentiendo) sonará como **"feelin"**
sing (cantar) sonará como **sin** (pecado)

La clave para pronunciar [ŋ] correctamente es elevar la parte trasera de su lengua y *no* la punta.

PRONUNCIANDO LOS SONIDOS
DE CONSONANTES FINALES

Consonantes Finales del Ingles . . .

Una consonante final en inglés es cualquier consonante que sea el último sonido de una palabra. Los sonidos de consonantes en inglés que terminan palabras son MUY importantes. Ellos pueden determinar el significado o la gramática de una palabra. Pronunciar las consonantes finales con cuidado le ayudarán a comunicar su mensaje correctamente y sin acento fuerte.

Nota: *Las palabras pronunciadas con consonantes finales a veces tienen a la "e" como la última letra. Cuando la "e" es la última letra en una* *palabra, es usualmente muda; una consonante es actualmente el último sonido. Ejemplos:*

made (hecho) **phone** (teléfono) **bite** (morder) **have** (tener)

Posibles Problemas de Pronunciación
Para Personas de Habla Hispana

En español, la mayoría de las palabras terminan en vocales. Es mas, la mayoría de las consonantes en español NO se encuentran al final de las palabras. En inglés, lo opuesto es cierto. La mayoría de las palabras terminan en consonantes. Como usted no está acostumbrado a usar consonantes finales en español, es muy probable que frecuentemente las omitirá al final de las palabras en inglés. Como consecuencia usted podría confundir a sus oyentes, al estos tener dificultad en entenderle

EJEMPLO 1: Su gramática sonará incorrectamente:

A. Verbos en tiempo pasado sonarán como verbos en tiempo presente:

stayed (se quedó) sonará como **stay** (quédate)
raced (compitió) sonará como **race** (competir)

B. Nombres plurales sonarán como nombres singulares:

cars (carros) sonará como **car** (carro)
hats (sombreros) sonará como **hat** (sombrero)

EJEMPLO 2: No estará diciendo la palabra señalada:

place (lugar) sonará como **play** (jugar)
card (tarjeta) sonará como **car** (carro)

EJEMPLO 3: Su oyente no le entenderá en absoluto:

"ca" sin consonante final no tiene significado. Usted puede estar diciendo "case" (caso), "came" (vino), "cake" (torta), "cane" (bastón), "cage" (jaula), "cape" (capa), o "cave" (cueva). Su oyente tendría que adivinar!

PRONUNCIANDO VERBOS EN TIEMPO PASADO (Page 159)

En inglés siempre se añade "ed" cuando escribimos los verbos en tiempo pasado. Esto es fácil de recordar! Pero al hablar en inglés, la terminación "ed" puede tener tres pronunciaciones distintas. A veces "ed" suena como [t], como en "stopped" [stɑpt] (se paró); a veces suena como [d], como en "lived" [lɪvd] (vivió); a veces suena como una nueva silaba, [ɪd], como en "loaded" [loudɪd] (cargado).

Posibles Problemas de Pronunciación
Para Personas de Habla Hispana

Como fue discutido en el capítulo sobre los sonidos de consonantes finales (pagina 152), en su mayoría las consonantes no se encuentran al final de las palabras en español. Por consiguiente, usted no esta acostumbrado a decir las consonantes finales en inglés. Esto hará que usted omita o pronuncie mal las terminaciones de verbos en tiempo pasado.

EJEMPLO 1: Verbos en tiempo pasado sonarán como verbos en tiempo presente:

> ***washed*** (lavó) sonará como ***wash*** (lavar)
>
> ***played*** (jugó) sonará como ***play*** (jugar)

EJEMPLO 2: Una nueva sílaba estará añadida incorrectamente a un verbo del pasado:

> ***lived*** [lɪvd] (vivió) sonará como ***lived-id*** [lɪvɪd]
>
> ***tapped*** [tæpt] (grabó) sonará como ***tap-id*** [tæpɪd]

EJEMPLO 3: Usted no estará diciendo el verbo en tiempo pasado señalado:

> ***played*** [pleɪd] (jugó) sonará como ***plate*** [pleɪt] (plato)
>
> ***tied*** [tɑɪd] (ató) sonará como ***tight*** [tɑɪt] (apretado)

Esto puede parecerle confuso pero no se preocupe! Tenemos buenas noticias! En este capitulo le enseñarémos tres reglas faciles que lo ayudarán a pronunciar los verbos en tiempo pasado correctamente. Usted aprenderá cuando "ed" suena como [t], [d], o [ɪd]. ¡Si aprende las reglas, no tendrá problemas!

PRONUNCIANDO PLURALES,
VERBOS DE TERCERA PERSONA,
POSESIVOS, Y CONTRACCIONES

Cuando se escribe en inglés, la letra "s" al final de palabras sirve para distintos propositos. La "s" se utiliza para formar nombres plurales (hats, dogs); verbos en la tercera persona singular (he likes; she eats; nombres posesivos (my friend's house; the dog's collar), y contracciones (it's late; he's here). Como ha visto, la "s" es una letra muy versatil del inglés. Es importante aprender sus distintos sonidos!

Al hablar inglés, la terminación "-s" puedo tener tres distintas pronunciaciones. Puede sonar como [s], como en "hats" [hæts]; [z], como en "tells" [tɛlz]; o como la nueva sílaba [ɪz], como en "roses" [rouzɪz].

Posibles Problemas de Pronunciación
Para Personas de Habla Hispana

Una vez mas, personas de habla hispana tienen la tendencia de no pronunciar las consonantes finales lo cual resulta en omisiones o en faltas de pronunciación de la "s" al final de las palabras. Esto hará que usted no sea entendido o confunda a sus oyentes.

EJEMPLO 1:   Nombres plurales sonarán como nombres singulares:

two books   (dos libros)   sonará como   **two book**   (dos libro)

EJEMPLO 2:   El tiempo de tercera persona singular será incorrecto:

he eats   (el come)   sonará como   **he eat**   (el como)
she sings   (ella sings)   sonará como   **she sing**   (ella cantamos)

EJEMPLO 3:   Posesivos y contracciones serán omitidas:

Bob's house   sonará como   **Bob house**
he's right   sonará como   **he right**

EJEMPLO 4:   Usted no dirá su palabra señalada:

my eyes   (mis ojos)   sonará como   **my ice**   (mi hielo)
Sue sings   (Sue canta)   sonará como   **Sue sinks**   (Sue se hunde)

Usted seguramente se estará preguntando si habrán reglas que lo ayuden a pronunciar la "s" correctamente en todas estas distintas posiciones. La respuesta es sí! En este capítulo usted aprenderá como pronunciar "s" cuando forma plurales, tercera persona singular del presente, posesivos y contracciones. Estudie las reglas y oiga cuidadosamente las cintas magnetofónicas. Usted pronto notará una gran mejoría en su pronunciación!